1,OO1 PEARLS OF FISHING WISDOM

"Many men go fishing all of
their lives without knowing that
it is not fish they are after."
    —Henry David Thoreau

1,001 PEARLS OF FISHING WISDOM

Advice and Inspiration for

Sea, Lake, and Stream

EDITED AND INTRODUCED BY
NICK LYONS

Skyhorse Publishing

Skyhorse Publishing books may be purchased in bulk at special discounts for sales promotion, corporate gifts, fund-raising, or educational purposes. Special editions can also be created to specifications. For details, contact the Special Sales Department, Skyhorse Publishing, 307 West 36th Street, 11th Floor, New York, NY 10018 or info@skyhorsepublishing.com.

Skyhorse® and Skyhorse Publishing® are registered trademarks of Skyhorse Publishing, Inc.®, a Delaware corporation.

Visit our website at www.skyhorsepublishing.com.

10 9 8 7 6 5 4 3 2

Background photos courtesy of Thinkstock from Comstock, Design Pics, Hemera Technologies, Ingram Publishing, iStockphoto, Jupiterimages, Photodisc, and Photos.com.

Library of Congress Cataloging-in-Publication Data is available on file.

ISBN: 978-1-62087-175-1

Printed in China

Contents

INTRODUCTION

I began to fish at such an early age that I have no memory of how or when I started. I only know that from as long as I can remember, I liked to catch anything that moved—frogs, grasshoppers, crayfish, newts, and the shiners and bluegill that lived in South Lake, near my grandfather's hotel. Later, I developed an uncanny memory for specific trips, specific lakes or creeks, and even for most of the large or difficult fish I caught. I was always mad for fishing.

But if I have been addicted to a wide range of different kinds of fishing, I have also for many years been mad for the words of fishing. It was not always so. Throughout my teens I read all those outdoor magazines, rarely books, and the magazines chiefly for their irresistible photographs. Books often seemed too long, rather dull. Gradually that changed and by my twenties I was as passionate about books and words as I was about the fishing itself. I had quietly fallen in love with all manner of printed matter, books first, and that included for the first time those wise, pithy, observant, speculative, hilarious, practical stories and comments about angling: about the fish themselves, the places where it all takes place, its technology, and the philosophical implications of it all.

This may well be because a good part of my professional life has been connected to words, ever since I wrenched my life out of one path and put it in another that led to teaching books, editing books, and writing a lot myself, often about fishing. Words, for nearly sixty-five years, have been as essential to my life as fishing—and fishing has been absolutely essential.

So it has been a pleasure for me to cobble together these 1,001 comments on fishing in many of its varied modes. "Pearls" they are to me—bright and valuable—and they have helped define for me the diversity of the angling experience. Some have come from my "commonplace books"—notebooks I keep to record memorable passages from my reading—and some from books I edited or read for pleasure; recently I have been able to find new ones disengaged from their original sources, from that modern tool, the Internet, which I have grown to use so late in my life. Often these latter words came from people who were just names to me, some of whom I had never heard of, but I could not resist the wisdom of their words.

Some of the comments herein are full of practical good sense and others enduring wit and shrewd observation. Often enough, held against their neighbors, they are full of delicious contradictions—one affirming without reservation or doubt that body color on a fly is of no concern to a trout, the next that it is all that finally matters. Many are perfectly memorable. In some the fishing passion is defined brilliantly; in others it is teased (or worse) for its absurdity. I like some for their humor, others for their criticism, a few even for their outright hogwash. I have tried to order them here—starting with "Origins" and progressing to more philosophic matters.

For some authors herein, I might have taken whole chapters from their books—A. J. McClane, Ray Bergman,

Introduction

Lee Wulff—replete fishermen who spoke from broad experience, or Lefty Kreh, a master of tips on everything from knots to casting; others—like Arnold Gingrich, Ted Leeson, Howell Raines, Roderick Haig-Brown, Tom McGuane, and a dozen others—edge fishing toward its more literary chances. We especially owe Holly Morris a special debt for encouraging and collecting a brilliant group of women anglers in her two pathbreaking anthologies: *Uncommon Waters* and *A Different Angle*. Joan Wulff is not only one of the great casters and teachers of casting but one of the best examples of why the notion of fishing as a male sport is such nonsense.

I hope in all cases here, the comments in this book will send you to the original books noted in the bibliography or to some further knowledge of authors still new to me. Mostly, I hope they will bring you some joy and, yes, some true wisdom that will make fishing more fun and more understandable.

—Nick Lyons
August 2012

ORIGINS

How this sport fishing began and how each of us began to fish are probably intertwined and, to me, endlessly interesting. Originally, of course, most fishing was done to acquire food, as it clearly still is, but something in the process of inducing a fish to be caught on a hook was clearly such fun to some of the first anglers that they began to develop ways subtler than the net to pursue this quarry. Lures, special baits, feathers tied to hooks, lines, and reels and rods developed especially for this human activity all helped. And then, as with all sports, rules or codes developed.

Each of us began differently—some, as I did, as very young children with the barest of equipment, and some as adults when the first rod was not a willow branch but a graphite wand costing the better part of a thousand dollars. It is amazing to me how many ways we diverge in the way we came to fishing, but even more amazing is how much we all overlap. Often the passion for it is so sudden and so deep—as in the case of the great Russian writer, Aksakov—that we think, with Walton, that some of us are "born so" or that there's an angling gene and we have it in spades.

Our tradition is that of the first man who sneaked away to the creek when the tribe did not really need fish.

—Roderick L. Haig-Brown,
A River Never Sleeps (1946)

[The fishermen] have planned a snare for the fish, and get the better of them by their fisherman's craft. They fasten red (crimson red) wool around a hook, and fix onto the wool two feathers which grow under a cock's wattles, and which in colour are like wax.

—Claudius Aelianus,
On the Nature of Animals (third century A.D.)

Angling is somewhat like poetry, men are to be born so . . .

—Izaak Walton, *The Compleat Angler* (1653)

4

Origins

Unencumbered by the knowledge that women didn't fish, it was obvious to me then, at age five or six, that it was better to be the fisherman than the rower.

—Joan Wulff

. . . my coordination was so poor I did most of my fishing in trees. . .

—Dave Hughes

I came from a race of fishers, trout streams gurgled about the roots of my family tree.

—John Burroughs

Now that Trout are in my field of study, I much regret that I started life as an idiot.

—Christopher Camuto

I lived in perpetual hope of seeing that wayward shimmy of the bobber, then the quick dip and tug that signaled I had made contact with aliens. At that time in my life this was my social interaction.

—Lorian Hemingway, "Walk on Water for Me,"
*A Different Angle: Fly Fishing Stories
by Women* (1995)

What I remember most of my first fly-fishing experience is a lot of yeps and nopes directed at my questions, the fly line cinched tightly around my ankles after a bad cast, and a sunburn that bubbled the skin on the tops of my ears.

—Lorian Hemingway, "Walk on Water for Me,"
*A Different Angle: Fly Fishing Stories
by Women* (1995)

. . . no man is born an artist nor an Angler.

—Izaak Walton, *The Compleat Angler* (1653)

6

Origins

Angling may be said to be so like the mathematics
that it can never fully be learnt . . .
> —Izaak Walton, *The Compleat Angler* (1653)

. . . from when I was eight to when I was fifteen, what
I chiefly remember is fishing.
> —George Owell, *Coming Up for Air* (1939)

The gear, in a man's size small, was uncomfortable,
and "bug dope," as it was called, was greasy and
strong smelling. Because I loved being outdoors, I
thought of it as paying the price to get the rewards,
but I did not fish as often or as comfortably as a young
man my age might have done.
> —Joan Wulff

1,001 Pearls of Fishing Wisdom

I was born in the heart of Dixie and raised in the redneck way of fishing, which holds that the only good trip is one ending in many dead fish.

—Howell Raines, *Fly Fishing Through the Midlife Crisis* (1993)

Our dancing school, meanwhile, had become very successful. In 1952 I decided to leave . . . after realizing that if I didn't make a conscious break I might be there for the rest of my life. That would mean I would always miss spring trout fishing because of preparations for our June dance recital.

—Joan Wulff

I was young, I was cocky, and I didn't know what the hell I was doing. I kept casting and I kept getting hung up and the harder I tried the worse it got and the more frustrated I became until finally I was crazy.

—Joe Humphreys, *On the Trout Stream with Joe Humphreys* (1989)

Origins

In my family, a thirteenth birthday decided not whether a child was an adult but whether he or she would become a fisherman.

> —Janna Bialek, "Thoughts from a Fishing Past," *Uncommon Waters* (1991)

Like most boys, I had a mistaken tendency to think that the best fish were the furthest out.

> —Luke Jennings, *Blood Knots* (2011)

I have been a seeker of trout from my boyhood, and on all expeditions in which this fish has been the ostensible purpose I have brought home more game than my creel showed.

> —John Burroughs, *Locusts and Wild Honey* (1879)

There is a lot said and written about beginner's luck, but none of it came my way.

> —Roland Pertwee, "The River God" (1928)

9

My son got an inexplicable joy from casting his little spinning rod over the ditch into the woods and reeling the rubber casting weight back through the trees.
—Ian Frazier, *The Fish's Eye: Essays about Angling and the Outdoors* (2002)

When the beginner can cast his fly into this hat, eight times out of ten, at forty feet, he is a fly fisher; and so far as casting is concerned, a good one.
—Dr. James A. Henshall, *Book of the Black Bass* (1881)

Young anglers love new rivers the way they love the rest of their lives. Time doesn't seem to be of the essence and somewhere in the system is what they are looking for.
—Thomas McGuane, "Midstream," *An Outside Chance* (1990)

Origins

I had come late to fly fishing for trout . . . after the waste of some thirty-four years upon less exalted pursuits. I was immediately hooked. . . .
 —Robert M. Mengel, *Fly Fisherman's Odyssey* (1993)

One of the turning points of my life was when I got my first bait-casting outfit. This purchase, using some of the earnings from my boiled peanut sales, was the culmination of months of desire, conversation, study of outdoor magazines and comparative analysis of advertisements for rods, reels and lures. Finally, when I was ready to get serious, I turned to the Sears, Roebuck catalogue and placed my order for a four-foot Shakespeare rod and a Pflueger reel.
 —President Jimmy Carter, *An Outdoor Journal* (1988)

My fishing began with perch and pumpkinseeds.
 —Ernest G. Schwiebert, Jr., "Memories of Michigan"

I was resistant at first. I remembered summer
vacations as a child, fishing with my father in a tippy
aluminum rowboat on a lake in Wisconsin, snagging
weeds and getting sunburned.

> —Le Anne Schreiber, "The Long Light,"
> *Uncommon Waters* (1991)

I hoped, of course, that my son would eventually
develop an interest in fly fishing, but I wasn't going to
push him. Fly fishing isn't like that. Either it calls you or
it doesn't.

> —Mallory Burton, "The Emerger,"
> *Uncommon Waters* (1991)

I hooked myself instead of the fish; tangled my line in
every tree; lost my bait; broke my rod; until I gave up
the attempt in despair . . .

> —Washington Irving, *The Angler* (1820)

The thought of fishing sent me wild with excitement.
> —George Orwell, *Coming Up for Air* (1939)

Origins

"What do you want to do this afternoon, old man?" he asked.

"Fish," I said.

"But you can't always fish," he said.

I told him I could and I was right and have proved it for thirty years and more.

"Well, well," he said, "please yourself, but isn't it dull not catching anything?"

And I said, as I've said a thousand times since, "As if it could be."

—Roland Pertwee, "The River God" (1928)

. . . I fished every day in the slip of a back garden of our tiny London house. And, having regard to the fact that this rod was never fashioned to throw a fly, I acquired a pretty knack in the fullness of time and performed some glib casting at the nasturtiums and marigolds that flourished by the back wall.

—Roland Pertwee, "The River God" (1928)

To the fisherman born there is nothing so provoking of curiosity as a fishing rod in a case.
—Roland Pertwee, "The River God" (1928)

It is of record that when the Pilgrims went to King James for their charter they said to him they desired to go to the new world to worship God and catch fish.
—Samuel S. Cox

Ray Bergman—"The Dr. Spock to a whole generation of American fisherman."
—John McDonald

As a child my bedtime stories had not been of princes and dragons but of fishing.
—Lewis-Ann Garner, "One for the Glass Case," *Uncommon Waters* (1991)

Origins

I sometimes think the barefoot kid with the cotton line and crooked pole (not rod) has us all skinned a mile.
> —Dr. Webb J. Kelly, "Day Dreams,"
> *The American Angler* (May 1921)

Teach your children to fly fish early in their stream careers.
> —Art Flick, *Art Flick's New Streamside Guide to Naturals and their Limitations* (2007)

I learned how to fly fish in the hit-and-miss, trial-and-error way that makes things stick, and I learned patience, persistence, acceptance and probably a few other good things too.
> —John Gierach, *Another Lousy Day in Paradise* (1996)

If a new man is particularly attentive he can learn to fly fish in a half hour. But then he will go on learning as long as he fishes for trout.

—Arthur R. Macdougall, Jr., "Rods and Rods," *The Trout Fisherman's Bedside Book* (1963)

I didn't know it, but a radical change had taken place in my life. I had become a fisherman and would never ever be quite the same again.

—Jack Hemingway

Mr. Coolidge took to a fly. He gave the Secret Service guards great excitement in dodging his backcast and rescuing flies from trees.

—President Herbert Hoover

Origins

I was abstract and dreamy in the rest of my life,
sometimes dangerously so, but as a fisherman I was
an empiricist, grounded in fact.

—Lou Ureneck, "Born the Fish: A South Jersey Boy's
Life," *The New York Times* (September 7, 2007)

The agony and the ecstasy is a six-year-old boy trying
to go to sleep, knowing he's going fishing in the
morning.

—Frank P. Baron,
*What Fish Don't Want You to Know
An Insider's Guide to Freshwater Fishing* (2003)

Many of the most highly publicized events of my
presidency are not nearly as memorable or significant
in my life as fishing with my daddy.

—President Jimmy Carter

Beginners often believe the myth of patience. The best anglers I know are somewhat impatient. If they aren't catching fish, they try something different.

—John Barsness

Opportunity is ever worth expecting; let our hood be ever hanging ready. The fish will be in the pool where you least imagine it to be.

—Ovid, *Ars Amatoria* (2 A.D.)

Until relatively modern times the world of fly fishing was small enough that it did not produce a great number of public documents; the footprint it left on the larger culture was light and the trail not always easy to follow.

—Ted Leeson, Introduction to *The Fly Fisher's Craft: The Art and History* by Darrel Martin (2006)

Origins

In the Yuan period, the hermit fisherman became
the symbol of the unemployed scholar. . . . The true
hermit scholar fished for fish, not fame; others merely
pretended to fish while waiting to return to politics.

—Shengmu

I am convinced that the dancing lessons improved
my casting because they taught me to use my whole
body to back up my limited ten-year-old strength.

—Joan Wulff, *Joan Wulff's Fly-Fishing: Expert Advice
from a Woman's Perspective* (1991)

Anglers boast of the innocence of their pastime; yet
it puts fellow-creatures to the torture. They pique
themselves on their meditative faculties; and yet their
only excuse is a want of thought.

—Leigh Hunt

FISH AND THE WORLD
THEY INHABIT

How mysterious water, that other realm, can be! And how we must understand it if we are to understand anything pertinent about the creatures who live there. It is a first principle, of course, that we must understand something about the great variety of fish we pursue if we expect to fish for them successfully.

The species of fish are marvelously diverse. Some, like the pike, are so savage they will eat anything that moves; others, like carp, prefer a stationary dough ball that would betray itself if it budged. Which is really "pound for pound" the greatest fighter once hooked? Which much be pursued with the most cunning?

I know anglers who have sought scores of fifty different species and have learned to adapt their strategy and technique that number of times. I have caught fewer than two dozen species and probably no more than ten with genuine passion, but I have enjoyed each and have come to understand and appreciate that the differences are part of what makes fishing so endlessly appealing.

Fish and the World They Inhabit

Fish intrigue me. I'm awed by their sleek shapes, colorful variations, patterned scales. Even more, I'm drawn to their mysterious allure.

—Joseph Tomelleri, "The Greatest Fish You've Never Seen," *Montana Outdoors* (July/August 2002)

Quite possibly this is the key to fishing: the ability to see glamour in whatever species one may fish for.

—Harold F. Blaisdell, *The Philosophical Fisherman* (1969)

I once saw a trout drown a pike: The pike had taken the trout so awkwardly and far back in its jaws that it could not dislodge the fish and so could not close its mouth to breath.

—Brian Clarke

Under its own ideal conditions every fish I've mentioned is a worthy gamefish, and at one time or another every one has proved too hot for me to handle.
 —Roderick L. Haig-Brown, *Gamest Fish of All* (1956)

Most of the world is covered by water. A fisherman's job is simple: Pick out the best parts.
 —Charles Waterman

The flounder is a wholesome fish and a noble one, and a subtle biter . . .
 —Dame Juliana Berners

It is motion that gives the fish his first warning of danger.
 —Lee Wulff

Fish and the World They Inhabit

Trout lie with an eye to the food supply. Salmon lie where they find comfort and feel secure.

—Lee Wulff

[Bluefish] are greedy, undiscriminating, and seem never to have been warned against fishermen.
—William Humphrey, "Tumult on a Wild Shore," *Sports Illustrated* (November 7, 1977)

Someone once said trout only swim in beautiful places. The same certainly holds true for Atlantic salmon, steelhead, bonefish, and myriad other fish species fly fisherman pursue around the globe.
—Mike Fitzgerald, Jr., Foreword to *Fifty Places to Fish Before You Die* by Chris Santella (2004)

I salute the gallantry and uncompromising standards of wild trout, and their tastes in landscapes.

—John Madson

25

. . . there is great pleasure in being on the sea, in the unknown wild suddenness of a great fish; in his life and death which he lives for you in an hour while your strength is harnessed to his; and there is satisfaction in conquering this thing which rules the sea it lives in.

—Ernest Hemingway, "On the Blue Water: A Gulf Stream Letter" (1936)

The Carp is the queen of rivers—a stately, a good, and a very subtle fish.

—Izaak Walton, *The Compleat Angler* (1653)

Experiments with black bass have shown that these fish prefer red over all other colors . . .

—Vlad Evanoff, *2002 Fishing Tips and Tricks* (1999)

Hatchery fish have the same colours, but they always seem muted like bad reproductions of great art.

—Bill Barich, *The Sporting Life: Horses, Boxers, Rivers, and a Russian Ballclub* (1999)

Fish and the World They Inhabit

A trout is vulnerable to the fisherman because he eats.
—Vincent C. Marinaro, *In the Ring of the Rise* (1976)

The bonefish in shallow water is a fish without parallel—the minnow, pound for pound, not excluded.
—Brian Clarke

I'd read about craggy, sinewy sportsmen who discover untouched bass lakes where they have to beat off the pickerel with an oar, and the saber-toothed, raging smallmouth chase them ashore and right up into the woods.
—Jean Shepherd, "Hairy Gertz and the Forty-Seven Crappies," *In God We Trust, All Others Pay Cash* (1966)

. . . a gut-shot landscape is no place for wild trout.
—Tom Palmer, "Trout Habitat in the Blackfoot Country," *In Praise of Wild Trout* (1998)

In Britain, three times as much money is spent on fishing for carp and coarse fish as on trout and salmon . . .

—Robert H. Boyle

A trout river is like a book: Some parts are dull and some are lively.

—H. G. Tapply, *The Sportsman's Notebook* (1964)

I consider him (the Black Bass) *inch for inch* and *pound for pound*, the gamest fish that swims. The royal Salmon and the lordly trout must yield the palm to a Black Bass of *equal weight*.

—Dr. James A. Henshall, *Book of the Black Bass* (1881)

The fact that trout are clean feeders establishes two other facts; namely that their sense of smell is well developed and that all water in which trout can live is perfectly safe for the angler to drink.

—Charles Zebeon Southard, "Trout Fly-Fishing in America," *American Angler* (Summer 1916)

Fish and the World They Inhabit

Ling are ugly, with functional and predacious ugliness
that possibly evolved to scare their prey to death.

—Dave Hughes

The rudimentary nature of the trout's brain forbids any
assumption that it can reason or even think.

—Sparse Grey Hackle, *Fishless Days,
Angling Nights* (1971)

The weight of a fish is commonly its only title to fame.

—Henry David Thoreau

Some anglers consider the carp a fine fish; others
despise it. One fisherman tells you carp are very
difficult to catch; a second man says they're a cinch.
I think all of these people are right. The carp is all of
those things, depending on what you think of it, and
how and where you fish.

—Ray Bergman, *Fishing with Ray Bergman*, (1970)

But if the salmon and trout must be classified as elite in this mythical social structure then let the black bass be given permanent status as the working class of American gamefish. He's tough and he knows it. . . . He's a bass sax grumbling get-down blues in the bayou. He's a factory worker, truck driver, wild catter, lumberjack, barroom bouncer, dock walloper, migrant farmhand, and bear wrassler. And if it's a fight you're looking for, he'll oblige anytime, anywhere. Whether it's a backwater at noon, a swamp at night, or dockside at dawn, he'll be there waiting. He's a fierce-eyed, foul-mouthed, tobacco-chewing redneck who has traveled to every corner of the nation, paying his way and giving no quarter.

—Pat Smith, "Old Iron Jaw,"
Lamar Underwood's Bass Almanac (1979)

Fish and the World They Inhabit

Out of the mysterious, hurrying river rose a monster,
huge beyond belief, vicious-looking, majestic,
terrifying . . . Its sides were gleaming silver.
> —John Taintor Foote, *Change of Idols* (1935)

I don't know of any fish that gives as much pleasure to
as many fishermen as the ubiquitous striper.
> —Ellington White, "Striped Bass and Southern
> Solitude," *Sports Illustrated* (October 10, 1966)

. . . water that isn't fit for trout won't much longer be
fit for us.
> —Arnold Gingrich

The trout is not intelligent, even for a fish. How could
he be caught on flies at all, how could he—given his
excellent sight—be so terminally indiscriminating, if he
were intelligent?
> —Brian Clarke and John Goddard,
> *The Trout and the Fly* (1980)

S: Will I really know when one is on?
F: Will you ever! Blues strike like blacksmiths'
hammers.

—John Hersey, *Blues* (1987)

The honest, enthusiastic, unrestrained, wholehearted
way that a largemouth wallops a surface lure has
endeared him forever to my heart. Nothing that the
smallmouth does can compare with the announced
strike of his big-mouthed cousin.

—John Alden Knight, *Black Bass* (1949)

The sight of the big carp had given me a feeling in my
stomach almost as if I was going to be sick.

—George Orwell, *Coming Up for Air* (1939)

There's something elemental in the first sight of a
pike.

—Luke Jennings, *Blood Knots* (2011)

Fish and the World They Inhabit

The natural end of a trout is starvation—starvation brought about by blindness.
>—Frank Sawyer, *Keeper of the Stream* (1952)

Selectivity is a simple reflex pattern. The cycle of the season is an annual recurrent emergence of insect species, one after another from the river. When each appears it takes a little while before the trout get accustomed to seeing it. Finally they sample the new insect, find it is safe and palatable, and begin to take it regularly.
>—Ernest G. Schwiebert, Jr., "Twelve Lessons for a Trout-Fishing Friend" (1971)

In some waters I have found the largemouth bass a very good fighter, but as a rule it doesn't have the staying power of either a smallmouth or rainbow trout.
>—Ray Bergman, "Ray Bergman Says Goodbye," *Fishing with Ray Bergman* (1970)

1,001 Pearls of Fishing Wisdom

Trout memories are short, and the fish hate to leave good holding spots for long so stand your ground.
> —Jerry Gibbs, "Fishing's Top 40," *Outdoor Life* (September 2007)

Their brain is smaller than a pea, and no fish has ever had an original thought.
> —Buck Perry, "Fish Doctors: A Generation of Hard-to-Catch Bass," *Outdoor Life* (March 14, 2012)

The muskie is the tiger of our waters. The northern pike is the wolverine.
> —Sid W. Gordon

. . . my uncle Silas used to tell me when I was a boy, "The damn pike used to be as big as hippopotomassiz."
> —H.E. Bates, *Gone Fishing: An Anthology of Fishing Stories* (1995)

Fish and the World They Inhabit

It began for me with the capture of a catfish—the most personable and handsome catfish—in the black pool below Poskin's dam.
  —Ben Hur Lampman, *A Leaf from French Eddy* (1965)

If trout suffer keen anguish while being "played," what do they suffer with? Not with any such brain or nervous system as ours . . .
      —Odell Shepherd, *Thy Rod and Thy Creel* (1930)

Compared to permit, bonefish are merely apprentice ghosts . . .

                              —Bill Lambot

Of all the fish that swim the watery mead,
Not one in cunning can the Carp exceed.
  —Leslie P. Thompson, *Fishing in New England* (1955)

You can catch a panfish at the end of any trolley line.
                          —Jack Denton Scott

. . . the carp is a vegetarian, and when in the mood,
may be tempted by potatoes, corn, peas, and beans
as well as dough, breadcrusts, plum cake, and bits of
fruit and berries.

—Leslie P. Thompson, *Fishing in New England* (1955)

The great trout was stationary almost as a stone. . . .
Swift as the swallow, and more true of aim, the
great trout made one dart, and a sound, deeper
than a tinkle, but as silvery as a bell, rang the poor
ephemerid's knell. The rapid water scarcely showed a
break . . .

—R. D. Blackmore, "Crocker's Hole" (1895)

. . . a lean, mean, ugly, oily, snaggle-toothed fish called
northern pike.

—Le Anne Schreiber, "The Long Light,"
Uncommon Waters (1991)

Fish and the World They Inhabit

I look for fish in any likely water I see—harbors, rivers,
irrigation ditches, hotel-lobby fountains.
—Ian Frazier, *The Fish's Eye: Essays about Angling and
the Outdoors* (2002)

. . . when the Trout was opened in the kitchen, within
him was found, and sent upstairs to his captor upon a
salver, three coppers and a lock ticket.
—Patrick R. Chalmers, *At the Tail of the Weir* (1932)

. . . a man going to a pond (where it seems a pike had
devoured all the fish) to water his mule, had a pike bite
his mule by the lips, to which the pike hung so fast,
that the mule drew him out of the water, and by that
accident the owner of the mule got the pike . . .
—Izaak Walton, *The Compleat Angler* (1653)

Does a five pound brown really think that my tiny mélange of dubbing, hackle and thread is a work of art deserving detailed examination? No. That fish is after food. Nothing more. Nothing less.
—John Holt, "Death on the Musselshell," *On Killing: Meditations on the Chase* by Robert F. Jones (2001)

The best pike waters have a numinous, forbidding air.
—Luke Jennings, *Blood Knots* (2011)

No trout, except possibly a very old, very heavy, very wise trout, fights like a large carp.
—Steven J. Meyers, *San Juan River Chronicle* (1994)

Playing favorites, as I have done with trout and bass, is an inadequate ethic, in part because the favoritism is based on sentiments that keep shifting.
—Le Anne Schreiber, "Predilections," *On Killing: Meditations on the Chase* by Robert F. Jones (2001)

Anyone who knows fish knows that pound for pound any salt-water fish is far stronger, far more disinclined to be hauled in on a line than a comparable fresh-water fish.

—Louis D. Rubin, Jr.,
The Even-Tempered Angler (1983)

. . . the walleyed pike is well worth fishing . . . for the walleye puts up a fight and is a delectable dish on the dinner table, its flesh firm and well-flavored.

—Sid W. Gordon

I told him a yellow catfish that had looked to weigh forty pounds had nearly torn the paddle out of my hands that morning. It was true . . .

—John Graves, *Goodbye to a River* (1960)

From the fisherman's point of view, the sea trout is equal to the finest grilse that ever ascended Tay or Tweed, exceeding as he does, for gameness and pertinacity every other British fish.

—David Foster

Sea trout. Like all anadromous fish its "ways are dark and past finding out."

—Fitz James Fitz, "Sea Trout," *Fishing with the fly: Sketches by lovers of the art* by Charles F. Orvis (1883)

[The steelhead] can hurtle into the air a split second after he is hooked, and flash hugely out in the murk, like the sword Excalibur thrust up from the depths—at once a gleaming prize and a symbol of battle.

—Paul O'Neil, "Excalibur: The Steelhead," *Sports Illustrated* (March 11, 1957)

Fish and the World They Inhabit

Those who fish get to know and understand a river in a way few others can.
—W. D. Wetherell, *This American River: Five Centuries of Writing About the Connecticut River* (2002)

They say that a trout can't think but you won't convince me that this crafty old veteran didn't know what he was doing when he made his long, looping departure.
—Rene Harrop, "Encounter on the Flat," *Into the Backing: Incredible True Stories About the Big Ones that Got Away* by Lamar Underwood (2001)

The milt of a male carp, broiled like a sweetbread and served on toast, is a dish beyond compare!
—Leslie P. Thompson, *Fishing in New England* (1955)

. . . trout that doesn't think two jumps and several runs ahead of the average fisherman is mighty apt to get fried.
—Beatrice Cook, *Till Fish Do Us Part: The Confessions of a Fisherman's Wife* (1949)

Fish die belly upward, and rise to the surface. It's their way of falling.

—Andre Gide

There are those times when salmon play no part in the proceedings of a day that is ostensibly spent in their pursuit.

—Dale Rex Coman, *Pleasant River* (1966)

. . . crappie are favorites because the certainty of some kind of fishing action is far better than promised battles that never come.
—Keith Sutton, *The Crappie Fishing Handbook* (2012)

Fish and the World They Inhabit

Most anglers spend their lives making rules for trout, and trout spend their lives breaking them!
—George Ashton

Saltwater fish are much stronger than their freshwater counterparts.

—Lefty Kreh

The legend of the trout's sagacity . . . arises from man's conceit. If the trout can outwit us, the lords of creation, he must be superior to us in cunning.
—P. B. M. Allan, *Trout Heresy* (1936)

Trout are quite unaware of their exalted status.
—Harold F. Blaisdell,
The Philosophical Fisherman (1969)

Fish like an artist and per adventure a good Fish may fall to your share.
—Charles Cotton, *The Compleat Angler* (Part 2) (1676)

The surf: certainly one of nature's finest edges.
—Russell Chatham, *Dark Waters* (1988)

The bird thinks it a favor to give the fish a lift in the air.
—Rabindranith Tagore

Hardly anyone in this country fishes for carp, but I'll tell you this, carp are one of the premier gamefish around.
—Lefty Kreh, quoted in *Fishing Giants and Other Men of Derring-Do* by Robert H. Boyle (2001)

An undisturbed river is as perfect as we will ever know, every refractive slide of cold water a glimpse of eternity.
—Thomas McGuane, "Midstream," *An Outside Chance* (1990)

Fish and the World They Inhabit

. . . there are carriers and side-streams on the River Test on which falls of spinners can be so heavy at certain times of the year that the eels have been seen there, lying just below the surface and rising to spent flies just as trout do.
—Peter Lapsley, *River Trout Flyfishing* (1988)

. . . an organ chorus of red howler monkeys swinging over a jungle stream as the tarpon roll and splash in counterpoint . . .
—A. J. McClane, "Song of the Angler" (1967)

. . . blues are both butchers and gluttons. They're cannibals that will eat their young. They will eat anything alive. They have stripped the toes from surfers in Florida . . .
—John Hersey, *Blues* (1987)

All pikes that live long prove to their keepers, because their life is so maintained by the death of so many other fish, even those of his owne kind, which has made him by some writers to be called the tyrant of the rivers, or the freshwater wolf, by reason of his bold, greedy, devouring disposition.

—Izaak Walton, *The Compleat Angler* (1653)

. . . bluegills . . . ounce for ounce, there is no better scrapper in fresh water.

—Elmer Ransom, *Fishing's Just Luck* (1945)

. . . the small-mouth is probably more active in its movements, the large-mouth is more powerful.

—Dr. James A. Henshall,
Book of the Black Bass (1881)

Fish and the World They Inhabit

Pike . . . my friend brought the second partridge to the riverside, tied some big trebles in it and hove it into the hair with his pike rod so that it splashed into the water just where the other had disappeared. It was gone on the instant, and my friend landed a twenty-five pounder.

—Arthur Ransome, "Uncaught Fish,"
Rod and Line (1929)

The greediness of pike knows no bounds.

—Sergei Aksakov, *Notes of Fishing* (1847),
translated by Thomas P. Hodge (1997)

Of the pike:
It is a fish of ambush.

—J. H. Keene, *The Practical Fisherman* (1881)

On bass:
This is one of the American freshwater fishes; it is surpassed by none in boldness of biting, in fierce and violent resistance when hooked.
—W. H. Herbert (Frank Forester),
Fishes and Fishing (1850)

. . .no bass fisherman can pass up a half-sunk log.
—Dave Hughes

With steelheading sometimes you have to smell the skunk before you can taste victory.
—Austin McPherson, "The Gorge,"
Fly Rod & Reel Online (October 29, 2008)

Fish and the World They Inhabit

Salmon are my totem. My original call of the wild. They are role models for three of the traits I value most: tenacity, courage, and passion. I even met my husband in an Alaskan salmon smokery—our wedding rings are twin gold salmon joined at the tail.

—Jessica Maxwell, "Twelve Flew into the Cuckoo's Nest," *A Different Angle: Fly Fishing Stories by Women* (1995)

Only dead fish swim with the stream all the time.

—Linda Ellerbee

But if the salmon and trout must be classified as elite in this mythical social structure then let the black bass be given permanent status as the working class of American gamefish.

—Pat Smith, "Old Iron Jaw," *Lamar Underwood's Bass Almanac* (1979)

Although I have been studying it for quite a few years, I actually know nothing more about how a trout's vision compares to ours than I did when I started.
—Art Flick

Fish are our superior, in that they seem to know, although they really know very little, that one sure way to stay out of trouble is by keeping your mouth shut.
—Arnold Gingrich, *The Joys of Trout* (1973)

As to salmon, Walton scarcely speaks a true word about their habits, except by accident.
—Andrew Lang, Introduction to Walton's *The Compleat Angler* (1906)

Fish and the World They Inhabit

A river has no past or future; it is always new.
—Luke Jennings

With the right conditions, Nature herself provides the best and the cheapest way of producing trout, and will produce as many as the food in the river will support.
—Dermot Wilson, *Fishing the Dry Fly* (1970)

As I peered over the bank a good trout backed like a phantom into obscurity.
—Romilly Fedden, *Golden Days* (1919)

SOME HINTS ABOUT
WHY WE FISH

Frankly, I would not hazard a definitive answer as to why we fish. There are dozens of reasons, most of them so personal that one is tempted to say, with Russell Chatham, that there are as many as there are people who fish. Still, some explanations appear more frequently than others and we often find that we share them, more or less: the uncertainty of it all, the adventures it brings, the varieties of ways we pursue fish, the qualities it brings out in us, the closeness it puts us with nature. Now and again, a skeptic or moralist will even attribute some of the basest reasons to our love of fishing. Ultimately, any true understanding of why we do it will usually come after years of experience on the water. Private and personal such reasons may be, but I'm sure you'll find hints of your own in the diverse comments that follow.

Some Hints About Why We Fish

. . . there has ever been a delightful uncertainty attending the angler's art, and therein lies one if its chiefest charms.

—Dr. James A. Henshall, *Book of the Black Bass* (1881)

I am having trouble explaining trout fishing to my city friends. They think it is either idleness or blood lust, and can't imagine why I spend so much time in the pursuit.

—Le Anne Schreiber, *Midstream* (1990)

There are some things, of course, that have always defied all forms of rationalization, and probably always will. Love, for instance. And faith, maybe. . . . Perhaps it's as futile and as foolish to ask "Why fly fishing?" as it is to ask "Why jazz?" As Fats Waller said: "Lady, if you've got to ask, you'll never know."

—Arnold Gingrich, *The Well Tempered Angler* (1965)

. . . fishing which lacks at least a trace of challenge will have more than a trace of boredom.

—Dave Hughes

There are as many reasons why and ways to fish as there are people who do it.

—Russell Chatham, *Dark Waters* (1988)

Here I'll make a confession, or rather two . . . nothing has given me quite such a kick as fishing. Everything else has been a bit of a flop in comparison, even women.

—George Orwell, *Coming Up for Air* (1939)

Freud is famous for wondering, "What do women want?" He might have asked a much tougher question: "Why do men fish?"

—James Gorman, "A Rite That Bonds the Generations," *The New York Times* (June 22, 2001)

Some Hints About Why We Fish

All earth is full of happy things when the angler goes a-trolling!
—Thomas Tod Stoddart, "Trolling Song" (1839)

There is certainly something in angling that tends to produce a serenity of the mind.
—Washington Irving

The music of angling is more compelling to me than anything contrived in the greatest symphony hall.
—A. J. McClane, "Song of the Angler" (1967)

Perhaps all you can say is that there are great lapses or discrepancies in time; that and the simple if inexplicable fact that some people have fishing in their hearts.
—Russell Chatham, "Fishing: Mystiques and Mistakes," *Dark Waters* (1988)

1,001 Pearls of Fishing Wisdom

No fisherman ever fishes as much as he wants . . . this is the first great rule of fishing, and it explains a world of otherwise inexplicable behavior.

—Geoffrey Norman

I continually read of men who said they would be just as happy not catching trout as catching them. To me, that even then sounded pious nonsense, and rather more of an excuse than a statement of fact. No, I want to catch them, and every time I slip on my waders and put up a fly, it is with this in mind.

—Brian Clarke, *The Pursuit of the Stillwater Trout* (1975)

The stream keeps me from getting lost, and anytime I feel like being a fisherman again, the trout are there, sages themselves, the wise *roshi* that caught me by the way and taught me to love wildness.

—Christopher Camuto, "Caught by the Way," *In Praise of the Wild Trout* (1998)

Some Hints About Why We Fish

. . . the fisherman fishes. It is at once an act of humility and a small rebellion. And it is something more. To him his fishing is an island of reality in a world of dream and shadow.

—Robert Traver, *Trout Madness* (1960)

All Americans believe that they are born fishermen. For a man to admit a distaste for fishing would be like denouncing his mother-love or hating moonlight.

—John Steinbeck

Early on I decided that fishing would be my way of looking at the world. First it taught me to look at rivers. Lately it has been teaching me how to look at people, myself included.

—Thomas McGuane, *The Longest Silence* (1999)

When we fish, we are awake. We are attuned to the environment, to the world, to the reverence and wonder of life.
—Dan Baughman, "Fishing, Spirituality and Us," *Bow Narrows Blog* (February 16, 2012)

The great charm of fly-fishing is that we are always learning; no matter how long we have been at it, we are constantly making some fresh discovery, picking up some new wrinkle. If we become conceited through great success, some day the trout will take us down a peg.

—Theodore Gordon

I fish because I love to; because I love the environs where trout are found, which are invariably beautiful . . . and, finally not because I regard fishing as being so terribly important but because I suspect that so many of the other concerns of men are equally important—and not nearly so much fun.

—Robert Traver, *Anatomy of a Fisherman* (1964)

Some Hints About Why We Fish

With the exception of painting, nothing in this life has held my interest as much as fishing. Fishing with a fly, bait, a handline; I don't much care. Fishing in my estimation is not a hobby, a diversion, a pastime, a sport, an interest, a challenge, or an escape. It is a necessary passion.

—Russell Chatham, *Dark Waters* (1988)

People that have not been inoculated with the true spirit may wonder at the infatuation of anglers, but true anglers leave them very contentedly to their wondering, and follow their diversions with a keen delight.

—William Howitt, *The Rural Life in England* (1838)

Fishing is fundamentally a game of chance, and at heart we are all gamblers.

—Dorothy Noyes Arms

Take along with you a bag, a landing-net and a contented heart. You know the familiar haunts of the perch? Thither go, then.
—Patrick R. Chalmers, *At the Tail of the Weir* (1932)

In every species of fish I've angled for, it is the ones that have got away that thrill me the most, the ones that keep fresh in my memory. So I say it is good to lose fish. If we didn't, much of the thrill of angling would be gone.

—Ray Bergman

Ours is the grandest sport. It is an intriguing battle of wits between an angler and a trout; and in addition to appreciating the tradition and grace of the game, we play it in the magnificent out-of-doors.
—Ernest G. Schwiebert, Jr.

Some Hints About Why We Fish

My favorite thing about fishing is being able to just be. Being able to get myself as quiet inside as it is outside.

—Sabrina Sojourner, "Currents,"
Uncommon Waters (1991)

The charm of fishing is that it is the pursuit of what is elusive but attainable, a perpetual series of occasions for hope.

—John Buchan

. . . a trout fisherman is something that defieth understanding.

—Corey Ford and Alastair MacBain, Introduction to
Trout Fishing by Dan Holland (1949)

Fishing, with me, has always been an excuse to drink in the daytime.

—Jimmy Cannon

Fishing is about being alone on the other end of a stick plunged into eternity, into primordial life.
—Janna Bialek, "Thoughts from a Fishing Past,"
Uncommon Waters (1991)

Angling is extremely time consuming. That's sort of the whole point.

—Thomas McGuane

What sense is there in the charge of laziness sometimes made against true fishermen? Laziness has no place in the constitution of a man who starts at sunrise and tramps all day with only a sandwich to eat, floundering through bushes and briers and stumbling over rocks or wading streams in pursuit of elusive trout.

—President Grover Cleveland, "Defense of
Fishermen," *Saturday Evening Post*
(October 19, 1901)

Some Hints About Why We Fish

Trigorin, when asked what a great literary man thinks about when he is alone:
I love fishing. I can think of no greater pleasure than to sit alone toward evening by the water and watch a float.

> —Anton Chekhov, *The Seagull* (1896)

When you bait the hook with your heart, the fish always bites.

> —John Burroughs

I am not against golf, since I cannot but suspect it keeps armies of the unworthy from discovering trout.

> —Paul O'Neil

Managed to fall into the Ogden brook—in fact went
in without the slightest difficulty, amid applause from
the bank; discovered from my involuntary plunge that
the water is just as wet as last year, and if memory
serves, a trifle colder. Reached home in the evening,
cold, wet, tired and hungry. Nevertheless, had a most
glorious time.

—A. Nelson Cheney

The wildness and adventure that are in fishing still
recommend it to me.

—Henry David Thoreau, *Walden* (1854)

Put simply, the swooping hawk, the belling stag
and the rising trout connect you with nature, whose
rhythms and laws are unchanging. There is no
pity there, and no sentimental narrative, only the
knowledge that you are part of a continuum.

—Luke Jennings, *Blood Knots* (2011)

Some Hints About Why We Fish

Angling consists as much in a love of the peace of the country and of Nature as in the taking of fish.
    —Eric Taverner, *Trout Fishing from All Angles* (1929)

Fishing, unlike most competitive sports, is played against a field of anglers trying to all best a common opponent—a living creature looking for a meal.
    —Jason Holmer, "Huff's Post: Fish Don't Know Who's On the Other End of the Line" quoted by Greg Huff, *North American Fisherman* (October 19, 2011)

A trout's brain is very small. It is sometimes said that dry-fly fishermen "pit their brains against those of the trout." No-one has ever leveled a bigger insult at us.
    —Dermot Wilson, *Fishing the Dry Fly* (1970)

. . . the best angling is always a respite from burden.
    —Thomas McGuane, *The Longest Silence* (1999)

Your true angler is a solitary or gregarious animal, according to occasion and circumstance. When he finds a two-pound trout sucking in the duns under the alders on the opposite bank, he wants to be solitary—very solitary.

—William Carter Platts, *Angling Done Here!* (1897)

Yes, this sport fits me—physically, mentally, psychologically. Why do I love trout? For the same reasons men do.

—Joan Wulff, "Where I Want to Be"

There was a civil war in my innards for which I could negotiate no peace save when wading in the river with the fish sharing their cold, sweet, silver life, becoming for bird and kine and native passer-by merely a harmless feller in the creek.

—Ferris Greenslet, *Under the Bridge* (1943)

Some Hints About Why We Fish

Even if you didn't see any fish that day, that doesn't mean that the next day might not be the day. That's the way you think when you are chasing records.
> —Robert Cunningham, *Chasing Records: An Angler's Quest* (2012)

The only reason I ever played golf in the first place was so I could afford to hunt and fish.
> —Sam Snead

"I hear what you're talking about," said the wife. "But you will make no impression on Humphrey. As long as the fish rise to his bait, everybody is what he ought to be. Bless you, Casaubon has got a trout stream, and does not care about fishing it himself: Could there be a better fellow?"

"Well, there is something in that," said the Rector, with his quiet, inward laugh. "It is a very good quality in a man to have a trout stream."
> —George Eliot, *Middlemarch* (1874)

We who go a-fishing are a peculiar people. Like other men and women in many respects, we are like one another, and like no others, in other respects. We understand each other's thoughts by an intuition of which we know nothing. We cast our flies on many waters, where memories and fancies and facts rise, and we take them and show them to each other, and small or large, we are content with our catch.
—W. C. Prime, *I Go A-Fishing* (1873)

Nothing is more trying to the patience of fishermen than the remark so often made to them by the profane: "I had not patience enough for fishing!"
—Arthur Ransome, "Fisherman's Patience,"
Rod and Line (1929)

Some Hints About Why We Fish

Around the kitchen table the family gathers, and following my enthusiastic lead, admire the swelling flanks covered by big shining scales, the symmetrical lines of a body of no mean bulk, and the rather fetching little Mongolian mustaches depending from the sides of a rounding mouth that appears to be on the point of whistling a merry tune.

—Leslie P. Thompson, *Fishing in New England* (1955)

I would sacrifice a bass any day to see the show-stopping ostentation of an osprey's wing-flared, talons-first plunge, the splash and flash of his catching without a thought of release.

—Le Anne Schreiber, "Predilections," *On Killing: Meditations on the Chase* by Robert F. Jones (2001)

. . . most fishermen soon progress beyond the need to prove themselves and the desire to compile lists of statistics.

—Luke Jennings, *Blood Knots* (2011)

. . . in my mature years I find I got more of nature into me, more of the woods, the wild, nearer to the bird and beast, while threading my native stream for trout, than in almost any other way. It furnished a good excuse to go forth; it pitched one in the right key.

—John Burroughs, *Locusts and Wild Honey* (1879)

. . . he that hopes to be a good angler must not only bring a large measure of hope and patience, and a love and propensity to the art itself; but having once got and practiced it, then doubt not but angling will prove to be pleasant, that it will prove to be, like virtue, a reward to itself.

—Izaak Walton, *The Compleat Angler* (1653)

. . . fishermen value most the fish that are hard to take and value least those that are offered to everybody on a fishmonger's slab.

—Arthur Ransome, *Rod and Line* (1929)

Some Hints About Why We Fish

And if ye angler take fysshe, surely thenne there is
noo man merrier than he is in his spyryte.
>> —Dame Juliana Berners,
>> *The Book of St. Albans* (1486)

Fishing is marvelous . . . there is the irresistible urge
to tangle with the mysterious and unknown, to rely on
intuition and hunches.
>> —Katharine Weber, "Without a Backward Cast,"
>> *Uncommon Waters* (1991)

. . . for me, fly fishing is a great puzzle-solving
challenge.
>> —Jennifer Smith, "Cheeseballs and Emergers," *A
>> Different Angle: Fly Fishing Stories by Women* (1995)

A boy and his dad on a fishing trip—
there is a glorious fellowship!
>> —Edgar A. Guest, "A Boy and His Dad,"
>> *When Day is Done* (1921)

I have always been a catholic fisher: one who derives pleasure from catching, or trying to catch, fish of any sort, from waters still or flowing, fresh or salt.
—Oliver Kite, *Nymph Fishing in Practice* (1963)

Modern-day anglers restlessly travel the globe, fishing new places, catching new species, meeting new people, imbibing new experiences and endlessly looking for, well, something.
—James R. Babb, "Around the Fire," *Gray's Sporting Journal* (February/March 2005)

If indeed, you be an angler, join us and welcome, for then it is known to you that no man is in perfect condition to enjoy scenery unless he have a fly-rod in his hand and fly-book in his pocket.
—W. C. Prime

Some Hints About Why We Fish

When you've got him on the bank you'll agree with me on this: That ketchin' pick'rel in a pond is seven kinds of bliss.

—Norman Jeffries, "Ketchin' Pick'rel,"
Fisherman's Verse (1919)

There is nothing like the thrill of expectation over the first cast in unfamiliar waters. Fishing is like gambling, in that failure only excites hope of a fortunate throw next time.

—Charles Dudley Warner

If you ever wondered why fishing is probably the most popular sport in this country, watch that boy beside the brook and you will learn. If you are really perceptive you will. For he already knows that fishing is only one part fish.

—Hal Borland

The take instantly validates our efforts, conferring a measure of definitiveness and closure to an enterprise otherwise riddled with uncertainty and inconclusiveness. Few things in life, I think, have this to offer.

—Ted Leeson, *The Habit of Rivers* (1994)

It's just that the longer that I fish, the more I long for simplification and lightness.

—Tom Sutcliffe, MD, *Reflections on Fishing* (1990)

I have learned that I am also a person who has to be able to go fishing whenever I can and for as long as I want to go. It is a silly thing, but there it is.

—Howell Raines,
Fly Fishing Through the Midlife Crisis (1993)

Some Hints About Why We Fish

The fisherman has a harmless, preoccupied look; he is a kind of vagrant, that nothing fears. He blends himself with the trees and the shadows. All his approaches are gentle and indirect. He times himself to the meandering, soliloquizing stream; he addresses himself to it as a lover to his mistress; he woos it and stays with it till he knows its hidden secrets.

—John Burroughs

The fishermen know that the sea is dangerous and the storm terrible, but they have never found these dangers sufficient reason for remaining ashore.

—Vincent Van Gogh

I don't fish in order to sit atop some predatory or evolutionary hierarchy. I fish to hook into an entirety. I fish to trade self-consciousness for creek-consciousness and self-awareness for rise-awareness. I fish to don dumb-looking but functional waterproof togs and even dumber-looking but functional facial expressions. . . .

—David James Duncan, "Stone. Water. Insect. Fish. Sunlight." *Los Angeles Times* (April 20, 2004)

Why are you obsessed with fighting? Stick to fishing from now on.

—Tim Rice, lyric from *Jesus Christ Superstar* (1971)

One of the greatest charms of angling is that of all the sports, it affords the best opportunity to enjoy the wonders and beauty of nature.

—J. J. Manley

Some Hints About Why We Fish

Fly rods in hand, they entered into the natural world, a world of risk, chance, raw energy, adventure.
—Harry Middleton, *The Earth is Enough: Growing Up in a World of Flyfishing, Trout & Old Men* (1989)

Perhaps fishing is, for me, only an excuse to be near rivers. If so, I'm glad I thought of it.
—Roderick L. Haig-Brown,
A River Never Sleeps (1946)

I still don't know why I fish or why other men fish, except that we like it and it makes us think and feel.
—Roderick L. Haig-Brown,
A River Never Sleeps (1946)

. . . what fishing ought to be about: using the ceremony of our sport and passion to arouse greater reverberations within ourselves.
—Thomas McGuane, *The Longest Silence* (1999)

A FEW WORDS ABOUT EQUIPMENT

Most anglers more than sixty years ago started with the simplest of equipment, much like that which I began to fish with: an alder branch, a yard or so of twine, a bobber, a hook. The outfit worked for the pumpkinseeds and perch I sought. But there has been a stunning proliferation of tackle this past half century and much of it is excellent and, for basic use, inexpensive.

The tools of angling can make all the difference in how successful we are: the right rod for you or for the kind of fishing you do; a reel with a smooth casting mechanism; a line or leader subtle enough not to frighten the fish you're after but strong enough to hold it; and so much more. Some tackle is very expensive, some much less so. Which to choose? Some anglers can't get enough equipment. Some have learned to choose with care. A lot of serious anglers have thought hard about these matters, and their revelations are often hugely helpful, sometimes even amusing.

A Few Words About Equipment

Logic class—the shorter you are, the more a longer rod will do for you.

—Joan Wulff, *Joan Wulff's Fly-Fishing: Expert Advice from a Woman's Perspective* (1991)

Reels are not made to be oiled. They are made to be greased.

—Sid W. Gordon

The reason for the jig's attraction probably is that most crustaceans and mollusks are bottom dwellers that hop when disturbed.

—A. J. McClane

Definition of a fly rod—an antenna, which transmits peace, tranquility, excitement, fellowship and most of all, an awareness and appreciation for the outdoors.

—Roderick L. Haig-Brown

1,001 Pearls of Fishing Wisdom

Keep your hooks sharp.

—Wise advice

When your leader is properly balanced, you should be able to take the butt end between your fingers and cast it straight out. No line, no rod, just leader.

—A. J. McClane

An old wool or heavy cotton sock makes a handy reel bag.

—Vlad Evanoff, *2002 Fishing Tips and Tricks* (1999)

For the beginning fisherman . . . the problem of rods, lines, reels and leaders can be quite complicated and needlessly expensive . . .

—Sid W. Gordon

A visit to a first-class fishing-tackle shop is more interesting than an afternoon at the circus.

—Theodore Gordon

A Few Words About Equipment

There he stands, draped in more equipment than a
telephone lineman, trying to outwit an organism with
a brain no bigger than a breadcrumb, and getting licked
in the process.

—Paul O'Neil

. . . one of the pitfalls of falling in love with old bamboo
fly rods was that there was no end to the number you
could collect.
—George Black, *Casting a Spell: The Bamboo Fly Rod
and the American Pursuit of Perfection* (2006)

Fly tackle has improved considerably since 1676, when
Charles Cotton advised anglers to "fish fine and far
off," but no one has ever improved on that statement.
—John Gierach, *Fly Fishing in the High Country* (2004)

1,001 Pearls of Fishing Wisdom

An angler, sir, uses the finest tackle, and catches his
fish scientifically—trout for instance—with the artificial
fly, and he is mostly a quiet, well-behaved gentlemen.
A fisherman, sir, uses any kind of 'ooks and lines, and
catches them any way; so he gets them it's all one to
'im, and he is generally a noisy fellah, sir, something
like a gunner.

—Dr. George Washington Bethune

Some fishermen think that any rod they buy and pay
for should stand any form of abuse, and if it does not,
the rod-maker is blamed and his work decried.

—Henry P. Wells, "Fly Rods and Fly Tackle" (1885)

Your whole being rests lightly on your float, not
drowsily: very alert, so that the least twitch of the float
arrives like an electric shock.

—Ted Hughes

A Few Words About Equipment

"I'll fish fiberglass," Sparse muttered behind his steel-rimmed spectacles, "the morning after some concertmaster plays a concerto at Carnegie Hall on a plastic violin!"

—Ernest G. Schwiebert, Jr., *Trout* (1978)

Again, let me remind you that rod action is an elusive and variable thing, refusing to be encompassed by exact definition.

—John Alden Knight, *Field Book of Fresh-Water Angling* (1944)

Every saltwater tackle box should contain a piece of emery cloth in it. It comes in very handy for touching up the point of a hook which has become dulled. It can also be used to remove rust from hooks, lures, knives, pliers, and other tools.

—Vlad Evanoff, *2002 Fishing Tips and Tricks* (1999)

But there's one suit I'd not trade you
Though it's shabby and it's thin,
For the garb your tailor made you:
That's the tattered,
Mud-bespattered
Suit that I go fishing in.

—Edgar A. Guest,
"The Fishing Outfit," *Just Folks* (1917)

Gone are the days of vulcanized rubber and neoprene
waders that were effectively like fishing in a really
heavy-duty trash bag—waterproof but uncomfortable.
—Tim Daughton, "Layering for Warmth and Comfort,"
Orvisnews.com (December 20, 2011)

Sensitive rods help detect more light-biting crappie.
—Keith Sutton, *The Crappie Fishing Handbook* (2012)

A Few Words About Equipment

The world that rod makers populate is a classic subculture, a recondite corner of the larger culture of fishing.

—George Black, *Casting a Spell: The Bamboo Fly Rod and the American Pursuit of Perfection* (2006)

It is amusing and even wonderful, what an amount of such stuff an ardent, green angler, with a flush pocket, can collect. As he grows older in the art, of course he throws it away, or imposes it as a present on someone no less verdant than he was himself a few summers before . . . .

—Thaddeus Norris

The Essentials of a Good Fly-Hook: The temper of an angel and penetration of a prophet; fine enough to be invisible and strong enough to kill a bull in a ten-acre field.

—G. S. Marryat

Looking good on the stream don't mean a thing to the trout.

—Jimmy D. Moore

We have been oversold on the short rod.
—Vincent C. Marinaro, *In the Ring of the Rise* (1976)

Put backing on your line, even if you never use it. It helps you dream.

—Jimmy D. Moore

The rod to strike, when you shall thinke it fit,
The line to lead the fish with wary skill.
The float and quill to warne you of the bit;
The hooke to hold him by the chap or gill,
Hooke, line, and rod all guided to your wit.
—John Dennys, *The Secrets of Angling* (1613)

A Few Words About Equipment

Lest the reader become too discouraged let me say
that one can fish beautifully with a rod that is not
perfection, but at the expense of undue physical
exertion.

—Eugene Connett, *Any Luck?* (1933)

Merely chopping the bottom off a long rod does not
result in a good short one.

—A. J. McClane, *The Compleat McClane*, (1988)

. . . the things that concern the float are all the fish you
are busy imagining.

—Ted Hughes

A good fly-rod is worth every cent you pay for it—
and more; also it should be said that good tackle of
any sort is not only its own reward but is absolutely
essential if you would have the best of the sport.

—Samuel G. Camp, *The Fine Art of Fishing* (1911)

1,001 Pearls of Fishing Wisdom

One of the few smart things I have ever done was to lay in a last-minute supply of Perfects that will last me my lifetime no matter how cleanly I live.

> —Leonard M. Wright, Jr., *Fishing the Dry Fly as a Living Insect* (1972)

. . . when I fly off on a fishing trip, my first carry-on bag has all my fishing gear . . .

> —Bill Lambot

The joy of owning fine tackle is so great that it is often difficult to distinguish between basic needs and the urge to possess that which delights the sensitivities.

> —Harold F. Blaisdell, *The Philosophical Fisherman* (1969)

If you cannot cast well within an entry-level, hundred-dollar rod chosen at random in the local tackle shop, then you need more lessons and practice. . . . You cannot buy tighter loops and greater accuracy.

> —Art Scheck, *A Fishing Life is Hard Work* (2003)

A Few Words About Equipment

If a fishing lure or accessory sounds too good, it probably is.

—Wade Bourne, *Basic Fishing* (2011)

A line must always be fastened securely to the inside of the spool. If you forget once and a fish strips the reel naked, you deserve several kicks. If you forget a second time, you are not worth kicking.

—Eric Taverner and John Moore, "Thoughts," *The Angler's Weekend Book* (1949)

The ideal trolling rod should have just enough bow in it at trolling speed so that when a fish strikes, the rod can naturally arc far enough to absorb the shock and set to the hook.

—Jack Denton Scott

You don't go deer hunting with a .22 rifle; fish enough and some day you're going to hook a trophy—and maybe land it, if you have the right equipment.
>   —A. K. Best, Interview with D'Arcy Egan, Cleveland.com (January 10, 2008)

Jigs are my favorite crappie lures.
>   —Keith Sutton, *The Crappie Fishing Handbook* (2012)

Early fly tying directions will always be contentious and challenged. The fewer the facts, the stronger the opinions.
>   —Darrel Martin, *The Fly Fisher's Craft: The Art and History* (2006)

Prepare your tackle! When you hook a big fish, it is impossible to retie or change a leader.
>   —Jim Chapralis

A Few Words About Equipment

Stiffness or softness of a rod has little bearing on the matter of fighting a trout on a delicate leader.
-Vincent C. Marinaro, "The Hidden Hatch,"
In the Ring of the Rise (1976)

A few dollars for a spool of line and one or two evenings spent bench testing is nothing compared to the cost of a trip to the Rogue River just to see the steelhead get away.
—Lindsey Philpott, *The Complete Book of Fishing Knots, Leaders, and Lines* (2008)

The bureaucracy of fly-fishing is supposed to serve you, not the other way around; the point, in the end, is not the gear.
—Ian Frazier, "Lighten Up,"
Outside Magazine (July 1, 2000)

1,001 Pearls of Fishing Wisdom

Let each use that rod which to him afford the most pleasure, and for him that rod is best, whether it be forty feet long or two.

—Henry P. Wells

What is most important is not the equipment or materials, it is the angler.

—Charles Jardine, Foreword to *Dynamic Nymphing: Tactics, Techniques, and Flies from Around the World* by George Daniel (2011)

[I]n regard to length and weight of rod and line, the grand point is to find *balance*.

—John Younger, *River Angling for Salmon and Trout* (1840)

As to patterns, I recommend buying flies locally, wherever you are fishing.

—Stu Apte, "World's Greatest Brown Trout Dry Fly Stream," *Field & Stream* (May 1972)

96

A Few Words About Equipment

The man who coined the phrase "Money can't buy happiness" never bought himself a good fly rod!
　　　　—Reg Baird, from his video *Labrador Trout*

The most indispensable item in any fisherman's equipment is his hat. This ancient relic, with its battered crown and well-frayed band, preserves not only the memory of every trout he caught, but also the smell.
　　　　—Corey Ford, "Tomorrow's the Day" (1952)

He who ties his own flies and makes his own rods and tackle will have a keener personal interest in his pastime.
　　　　—Leroy Milton, "Getting out the Fly Books,"
　　　　　　Angling (1897)

TECHNIQUES AND
STRATEGIES

Each form of fishing has its own techniques and strategies, of course—and its own challenges. Bait casting, spinning, surf fishing, fly fishing—all require practice and skill. All, when better understood and mastered, will lead to better catches. Part of the whole process of fishing begins with the knowledge of the water you will be fishing and the habits of the fish that live in such a place, but significant improvement in your success will come from such a simple "pearl" as "Watch the birds" or how best to wade or approach your quarry. Casting farther and with more care will be essential at times, and so will how you retrieve a lure, how you set the hook and fight a fish, avoiding such bugbears (if you fly fish) as drag, and certainly choosing the proper lures or bait or flies are of the greatest importance. Some of the advice in this section comes from unknown anglers, but most comes from those professionals who know whereof they speak, and their words can make all the difference.

Techniques and Strategies

Fishing is no simple or trifling matter, but requires for its practice all sorts of instruments and accomplished knowledge of clever and ingenious tactics.

—Plutarch

The first principle in all fishing is simple: never let the fish know he's being fished for.

—Havilah Babcock

There will be no end to angling controversies for there is no one best way for everyone to fish.

—Lee Wulff, *Lee Wulff's Handbook of Freshwater Fishing* (1939)

But remember this—some of the best fly fishermen I've ever known were merely ordinary casters, while some of the best casters I've ever seen known were poor fishermen.

—Ray Bergman, *Trout* (1952)

. . . kinds of impediments which cause a man to catch
no fish . . .
tackle is not adequate
you do not angle in biting time
if the fish are frightened by the sight of a man
the weather is hot
if the wind is in the east

—Dame Juliana Berners

It is not easy to tell one how to cast. The art must be
acquired by practice.

—Charles F. Orvis

. . . the most common factor that betrays the trout is
its movement . . . movement equals fish.

—Brian Clarke and John Goddard,
The Trout and the Fly (1980)

Techniques and Strategies

Study the water before fishing it. Select the most advantageous spot to fish from. Remember that the obvious places in the hard-fished streams are less likely to produce than the tough spots which no one fishes.

—Ray Bergman, *Trout* (1952)

To fish, fine and far off, is the first and principal rule for Trout Angling.

—Charles Cotton, *The Compleat Angler* (Part 2) (1676)

Before you can ever become a distance caster you must understand the role of your line hand.

—A. J. McClane

Know which direction your fish is facing before you make a cast—then cast to its eating end.

—Lefty Kreh, *Lefty Kreh's Presenting the Fly: A Practical Guide to the Most Important Element of Fly Fishing* (1999)

False albacore like a fast-moving lure. . . . reel in as fast as you can turn the handle.
—Vlad Evanoff, *2002 Fishing Tips and Tricks* (1999)

When a bass strikes at the bug and misses, rest him a while before offering your lure again. Give him time to get back to his former position and begin wondering what that queer-looking bug was and how it got away.
—Joe Brooks, *Bass Bug Fishing* (1947)

There is absolutely no substitute for learning how bass react in the specific lake or river that you will regularly fish.
—Jerry Gibbs, *Bass Myths Exploded: Newest Ways to Catch Largemouths* (1978)

Techniques and Strategies

One of the most important principles of wading was discovered by Archimedes in a Roman bathtub. The weight of a body underwater is equal to its above-the-surface weight less the weight of the water it displaces.

—Lee Wulff

In waters where there are shrimp, one of the top lures is a small jig.
—Vlad Evanoff, *2002 Fishing Tips and Tricks* (1999)

Lakes with lots of cover can be difficult, since the bass can be almost anywhere. This is the time to cast and move, cast and move.
—Lefty Kreh, *Lefty Kreh's Ultimate Guide to Fly Fishing: Everything Anglers Need to Know* (2003)

Strike or do not strike when a salmon rises to a wet fly? *Do not strike! Do set the hook!*

—Lee Wulff

Walton without Cotton is like good manners without meat!

—Eric Taverner and John Moore, *The Angler's Weekend Book* (1949)

As a general rule, in spinning for most gamefish an erratic playback is usually more effective than a constant wobble or spin of the lure.

—A. J. McClane

Most fishermen use the double haul to throw their casting mistakes further.

—Lefty Kreh

I've had my share of hairy moments, always from the same mistake—misjudging the strength of the current.

—A. J. McClane

Techniques and Strategies

Take a plastic worm or eel and split the tail. This gives
the lure more wiggle and draws more strikes.

—Vlad Evanoff, *2002 Fishing Tips and Tricks* (1999)

. . . until man is redeemed he will always take a fly rod
too far back . . .

—Norman Maclean, *A River Runs through It* (1976)

Minor tactics are active, not passive.

—Ferris Greenslet

The stream before you is constantly changing. If
you are not flexible or confident enough to adapt to
changing conditions on the stream, you are sure to fail.

—Joe Humphreys, *Joe Humphreys's Trout Tactics* (1981)

. . . an angler should stay with a beautiful lake or a
grand stream long enough to get acquainted with it.

—Sid W. Gordon, *How to Fish from Top to Bottom* (1955)

. . . secretly I lament the hundreds [of fish] we never caught because we forever persisted in fishing only the likeliest holding water.

—Tom Sutcliffe, MD, *Reflections on Fishing* (1990)

Watch the birds.

—Dick Sternberg, "Fishing's Top 40," *Outdoor Life*

. . . a moderately fast retrieve will attract chain pickerel, northern pike, and muskellunge, whereas largemouth and smallmouth bass are more frequently caught by reeling slowly.

—A. J. McClane

I much prefer coaxing a fish to dash no more than ten feet for any lure. I do not believe in giving him too much time to look critically at a lure that is definitely a fraud.

—Sid W. Gordon

Never throw a long line when a short one will serve your purpose.
   —Richard Penn, *The Angler's Weekend Book* (1833)

[M]aking one's own hooks by hand provides insight into a craft where the tools and procedures have remained basically unchanged for thousands of years.
   —John Betts, Foreword to *The Fly Fisher's Craft: The Art and History* by Darrel Martin (2006)

There is no taking trout in dry breeches.
                                        —Cervantes

If you have a giant's strength, you mustn't use it like a giant. If you do you will never make a long or graceful cast with either trout or salmon rod.
             —George Dawson, "Fly Casting for Salmon," *Fishing with the fly: Sketches by lovers of the art* by Charles F. Orvis (1883)

109

It is virtually impossible for a fish to throw a hook on a slack line.
>—Vincent C. Marinaro, "The Hidden Hatch,"
>*In the Ring of the Rise* (1976)

Stay still for long enough at the waterside and things start to happen.
>—Luke Jennings, *Blood Knots* (2011)

You will probably spot just a piece of a fish first and your brain will have to fill in the rest of the fish from memory.
>—Tom Rosenbauer, *The Orvis Guide to
>Beginning Fly Fishing* (2009)

Light rods for larger fish are sporting only if they don't prolong the fight.
>—Paul Guernsey, *Beyond Catch & Release* (2011)

Techniques and Strategies

Fishing success breeds confidence and confidence breeds success. Start simple to build confidence. Then gradually move to other species and more advanced techniques.

—Wade Bourne, *Basic Fishing* (2011)

When dressing dry-flies, we must always keep in mind the fish's point of view rather than our own.

—Romilly Fedden, *Golden Days* (1919)

Always be ready for a strike. You must set the hook instantly when fishing with dry flies for brook trout, because the little fellows are gifted with the ability of sampling your attraction and discarding it about as fast as you can wink an eye.

—Leon L. Bean, *Hunting, Fishing, and Camping* (1942)

Confidence is the best lure in your tackle box.

—Gerald Swindle

1,001 Pearls of Fishing Wisdom

The first and the last object of the fly-fisher is to show as much of the fly to the fish as possible, and as little of everything else.

—Francis Francis

Be patient and calm—for no one can catch fish in anger.

—President Herbert Hoover

Don't bottom fish.

—Peter Lynch

See how he throws his baited lines about,
And plays his men as anglers play their trout.
  —Oliver Wendell Holmes, Sr., "The Banker's Secret,"
  The Poetical Works of Oliver Wendell Holmes (1850)

You must lose a flie to catch a trout.
  —George Herbert, *Jacula Prudentum* (1651)

Wading is inherently dangerous, and doing it well is more of an acquired skill than it appears. Trying to manage line while wading is an unnecessary risk. Do one, then the other.

—Bryan Eldridge, "6 Things Guides Do That You Shouldn't," Orvisnews.com (November 11, 2011)

If the line is too light, one might just as well cast with grocery twine.

—Sid W. Gordon

[W]hen it came to pure fishing savvy and practical streamcraft, those old guys were our equals—and maybe, sometimes, our superiors. I have no intention of abandoning modern fly fishing's technological luxuries, but I'd be foolish not to pay attention to what our Old Guy accomplished without them.

—Paul Schullery, *American Angler* (December 8, 2010)

Most fishermen fish a bass bug, fly or lure too fast . . .
—Sid W. Gordon

All avid anglers know fish are attracted to bubbles.
If you are using a hollow plastic tube jig on your line,
just break off a piece of Alka-Seltzer and slip it into
the tube. The jig will produce an enticing stream of
bubbles as it sinks.
—"5 Little-Known Fishing Secrets," *Reader's Digest*

If you want to actually catch fish during run-off, you
have to use a nymph.
—Ailm Travler, "Run-Off," *A Different Angle:
Fly Fishing Stories by Women* (1995)

If your eyesight is no longer so hot, use an old-
fashioned needle-threader to help thread line through
hooks.

—Keith Sutton

Techniques and Strategies

All record-setting anglers agree that they had to learn
their knots first . . .

—Lindsey Philpott

Practice will help your fingers remember the
moves . . .

—Lindsey Philpott, *The Complete Book of Fishing
Knots, Leaders, and Lines* (2008)

At night I try to drop my fly or floating lure as close as
I possibly can to their nighttime swirls or rises.

—Sid W. Gordon

A fly twitched slightly on the surface will raise trout all
day long on the much-neglected pools and long flats
where the dead-drift nymph or dry fly would seem
very dead indeed.

—Leonard M. Wright, Jr., *Fly Fishing Heresies* (1975)

An upstream dead drift is the most productive cast for larger trout.

—Craig Mathews,
Western Fly-Fishing Strategies (1998)

. . . blind fishing a spring creek where there is no surface activity is unproductive and accomplishes little but spooking the trout.

—Craig Mathews,
Western Fly-Fishing Strategies (1998)

But I know many tricks and I have resolution.

—Ernest Hemingway,
Santiago in *The Old Man and the Sea* (1952)

Ninety percent of all fishing knowledge is local knowledge.

—Lefty Kreh

Fishing a good spot under the wrong conditions is like lacing up your ice skates in July.
>—David DiBenedetto, *On the Run: An Angler's Journey down the Striper Coast* (2005)

. . . color is not as important as action.
>—A. D. Livingston, *Fishing for Bass* (1974)

[M]any fly fishermen still act as if the fish were deaf, blind, and stupid, which keeps anglers from having the kind of success they desperately want. A good fly fisher is always aware of his surroundings and how his place in them may be tipping off the fish that something's amiss.
>—Phil Monahan, "5 Keys to Stealth," Orvisnews.com (April 4, 2012)

Sometimes the best spots are just beyond your casting distance.
— Frank Hilton, "Shore Fishing Frustrations,"
Free Bass Lures (January 9, 2012)

[A] guide once told me the best way to practice is to stand in your yard on a rocking chair, have a friend roll a hula hoop in front of you, and practice tossing the fly through the moving hoop. If you can do that consistently, I reckon you'd satisfy most any flats guide.
— Buzz Bryson, "Making the Speed Cast,"
Fly Rod & Reel (January 2007)

Oh that I could do it all again with graphite!
— Joan Wulff, *Joan Wulff's Fly-Fishing:
Expert Advice from a Woman's Perspective* (1991)

Techniques and Strategies

Fly fishing is as much an affair of gestures as tactics.
—Christopher Camuto,
A Fly Fisherman's Blue Ridge (2001)

Opportunities are everywhere and so you must always let your hook be hanging. When you least expect it, a great fish will swim by.

—Og Mandino

The best fisherman in the world can't catch them if they aren't there.

—Anthony Acerrano

The one great ingredient in successful fly-fishing is patience. The man whose fly is always on the water has the best chance. There is always a chance of a fish or two, no matter how hopeless it looks.

—Francis Francis

If you pass your line neatly and well three times over a trout, and he refuses it, do not wait any longer for him: You may be sure he has seen the line of invitation which you have sent over the water to him, and does not intend to come.

—Richard Penn, *Maxims and Hints for an Angler and Miseries of Fishing* (1833)

Caution is a most valuable asset in fishing, especially if you are the fish.

—Anonymous

The number of people who can throw just sixty feet accurately or inaccurately belong to a regal minority.
—Vincent C. Marinaro, *In the Ring of the Rise* (1976)

Why bother with such as worms, when trout will strike at a floating feather, a red berry, or a pine matchstick.
—Arthur R. Macdougall, Jr., "Matchsticks and So On,"
The Trout Fisherman's Bedside Book (1963)

WAYS TO DO IT

It's hard to define exactly why one angler prefers to fish with a surf rod, another with a stubby bait-casting outfit, one through the ice, another at night, one on the bottom (with bait), and an increasing number with a fly rod (the richness of which we'll explore later). But all of us who fish have preferences—for one reason or another—and we all find a specific method most pleasurable to use. My old friend Angus Cameron, now deceased, loved both salmon fishing with a fly and flounder fishing with a bit of clam, and wisely noted how much stupid snobbishness there is in the world of fishing. For my money, it's an extremely wide-ranging sport and I'm very happy to share it with folk who fish in entirely different ways from the few I've chosen because they give me the most pleasure. And we can learn from those who take a different road, and certainly we can understand them better if we genuinely listen. Here are some ways many different anglers fish and what a lot of fun most of them have.

Ways to Do It

. . . an earthworm . . . is the best bait for all kinds of
fish.

—Dame Juliana Berners

The best way to fish is alone.
—Ellington White, "Striped Bass and Southern
Solitude," *Sports Illustrated* (October 10, 1966)

Weird stuff happens after dark. Fishermen run over
logs, scare off skinny dippers, hook bats, step off the
ends of docks, pour coffee in their laps, eat bait, and
on rare occasions, catch fish.
—Jim Mize, "Night-Fishing Tips,"
Field & Stream (February 1992)

And when he struck his first cod, and felt the fish
take the hook, a kind of big slow smile went over
his features, and he said, "Gentlemen, this is solid
comfort."

—Stephen Vincent Benet

This is night fishing . . . a gorgeous gambling game in which one stakes the certainty of long hours of faceless fumbling, nerve-racking starts, frights, falls, and fishless baskets against the off-chance of hooking into—not landing necessarily or even probably, but hooking into—a fish as long and heavy as a railroad tie and as unmanageable as a runaway submarine.

—Sparse Grey Hackle, "Night Fishing,"
Fishless Days, Angling Nights (1971)

A fisherman chooses his method to suit the mood that moves him. Some people must be constantly in motion, in pursuit of fish. Others sit and wait and they also fish.

—Dave Hughes

That is winter steelhead: long hours of cold, interminable work, punctuated with breathless moments of excitement.

—Steve Raymond, *The Year of the Angler* (1973)

Ways to Do It

Surf-casting is not a duffer's sport. And you are sure to catch many more fish from a boat.

— Negley Farson

Dapping is the most exciting way of fly fishing.

— Robert H. Boyle, *Dapping: The Exciting Way of Fishing Flies that Fly, Quiver and Jump* (2007)

But we, we locals, detested pier fishing. It meant a crowd; and that meant you lost the chief thin in surfcasting—the luxury of your own solitude.

— Negley Farson, *Going Fishing* (1943)

To a far greater degree than other kinds of fishing for pleasure, the art of bottom fishing involves the actual catching of fish.

— Louis D. Rubin, Jr., *The Even-Tempered Angler* (1983)

. . . left to his own natural instincts and his common sense, any man of reasonable intelligence and sensibility is likely to favor bottom fishing above all other forms.
—Louis D. Rubin, Jr., *The Even-Tempered Angler* (1983)

The art of bottom fishing is that of letting the fish come to the fisherman, instead of vice versa. . . . Bottom fishing, in short, is the Thinking Man's fishing.
—Louis D. Rubin, Jr., *The Even-Tempered Angler* (1983)

It is hoped for the roach pole, that it may achieve roaches.
—Patrick R. Chalmers, *At the Tail of the Weir* (1932)

The golden rule on the riverbank is—move slowly. And move smoothly.
—Brian Clarke and John Goddard,
The Trout and the Fly (1980)

Ways to Do It

Sleep came immediate, and with it vivid recollections of a bonefish tailing on hard sand.

> —Sam Sifton, "Silent Days on the Sea,"
> *The New York Times* (March 28, 2010)

The sea is a desert. You watch the water until your eyeballs are popping out, but no fish appear. And you go home with empty hands and an empty wallet, punished for your arrogance and your unjustifiable confidence—as you should be.

> —Robert Cunningham, *Chasing Records:*
> *An Angler's Quest* (2012)

Lie thou there, for here comes the trout that must be caught with tickling.

> —William Shakespeare, *Twelfth Night* (c. 1601)

In Minnesota, I'm haunted and taunted by the muskies that pass through my thoughts and trail just behind my lures. And I'm quite convinced that the mouths of the largemouth bass in Mexico are much bigger than they need to be.

—Jeff Simpson, "One Recipe Worth Duplicating,"
In-Fisherman (December 7, 2011)

The strike is the roach fisherman's art, for roach have tiny suspicious mouths and love to nibble at a bait or take it in and eject it so quickly that the movement scarcely shows in a quiver on the float.

—Roderick L. Haig-Brown,
A River Never Sleeps (1946)

. . . to master ocean fly fishing, nothing beats *time on the water*.

—Lou Tabory, *Inshore Fly Fishing* (1992)

Ways to Do It

To the tweedy followers of *Salmo salar* and *Salvelinus fontinalis*, such words as "black bass" soured on the tongue like domestic caviar.

—Pat Smith, "Old Iron Jaw,"
Lamar Underwood's Bass Almanac (1979)

. . . an important attribute in shoreline fishing for largemouths is a sensitive eye for the slight irregularities which are all that a bass needs to achieve concealment.

—Harold F. Blaisdell,
The Philosophical Fisherman (1969)

You can easily minimize a sport by coming at it with too sharp an angle in the manner of a technocrat.

—Jim Harrison, "Older Fishing,"
Astream: American Writers on Fly Fishing (2012)

A frog-fisher always looks down on the man who uses the mechanical lures, sneering that he is "fishing with machinery."

—Negley Farson, *Going Fishing* (1943)

I know of no more absorbing adventure than to wade slowly across some white tropic flat. Although the bonefisherman may go home empty-handed, if he has eyes to see and ears to hear he will be a silent observer of the myriads of sea creatures living out their destinies all about him.

—Stanley M. Babson, *Bonefishing* (1965)

Hunting and fishing are the second and third oldest professions, yet bonefishing is the only sport that I know of, except perhaps swordfishing, that combines hunting and fishing.

—Stanley M. Babson, *Bonefishing* (1965)

Ways to Do It

The floating bread-crust works! "Minor tactics" have come to carp fishing.

   —Leslie P. Thompson, *Fishing in New England* (1955)

You cannot, of course, fish for big carp in half a day. It takes a month.

      —H. T. Sheringham, *Coarse Fishing* (1912)

I cast across the pool and watched my Mepps flash its way back, looking like nothing that might occur naturally in the river. It nearly ran into one fish, which turned to look at it and then, slowly, eased back into position.

      —Nancy Lord, "Magadan Luck," *Uncommon Waters* (1991)

Fishing for barbell needs a greater expenditure of worms and faith than I have ever been in a position to afford.

   —Arthur Ransome, "My Barbel," *Rod and Line* (1929)

Eels call, on capture, for swift action, firmness of
character and a Finnish knife.
>—Arthur Ransome, "A Mixed Bag,"
>*Rod and Line* (1929)

A man who fishes habitually for carp has a strange
look in his eyes.
>—Arthure Ransome, "Carp," *Rod and Line* (1929)

. . . blunt emergence
of bullhead, his slow surge to the bait, glint
of the small, mucusoid eye—
sluggish black spasm of flesh,
he bites, and I haul him out,
but he does not die at once.
>—John Engles, "Bullhead," *Big Water* (1995)

Ways to Do It

. . . angling—rod and reel, troutline, jugline, grabbling, whatever—offers possibly our last link with the eternal verities of nature and pursuit. And no better fish to pursue than the one with whiskers.

—M. H. "Dutch" Salmon,
The Catfish as Metaphor (1997)

A cork bobs, a stick jerks up, and a fiery stickleback bristling, streaming, describes an unaccustomed arc through the air.

—Brian Clarke, *The Pursuit
of the Stillwater Trout* (1975)

I know literally thousands of fishermen, yet in all this multitude I can number only four men who can handle a bass fly rod the way it should be handled . . .

—John Alden Knight, *Black Bass* (1949)

To me, bream on a fly rod are as pretty fishing as a man can want, but there are times when they aren't worth working for.
—John Graves, *Goodbye to a River* (1960)

Purists really burn my ass. You can always tell when you've come across one. On the surface, his manners will be impeccable, but his low opinion of you will show through every feature and world.
—Angus Cameron, "What Burns My Ass," *Outside Magazine* (July 1, 2000)

In my opinion, the bluegill is one of the best fighters in the panfish category. He fights with spirit, speed and vigor right up to the finish. . . . Sometimes bluegills will rise to dry flies, but on the whole I find them more ready to take wet flies, streamers and nymphs.
—Ray Bergman, *Fishing with Ray Bergman*, (1970)

Ways to Do It

No friend of violent exercise, the Judge . . . simply
impaled a big hearty smelt on a bar hook and threw
it off the bridge . . . to swim around and drum up
business.

—Sparse Grey Hackle, *Fishless Days,*
Angling Nights (1971)

Nothing is like a Jitterbug strike. . . . A bass . . . grabs a
Jitterbug with a sudden violence that takes my breath
away even after seeing and hearing it hundreds of
times.

—Art Scheck, *A Fishing Life is Hard Work* (2003)

[T]he hard diving tuna liberates the brute instinct in a
man.

—Zane Grey, "Big Tuna," *The Best of Field & Stream:*
100 Years of Great Writing (1995)

The best fishermen I know try not to make the same mistakes over and over again; instead they strive to make new and interesting mistakes and to remember what they learned from them.

　　—John Gierach, *Fly Fishing the High Country* (1999)

. . . night fishing has its particular compensation: The sea's neon phosphorescence lights up the stripers as if they're electric.

　　　　　　　　　　　—Margot Page, "The Island,"
The Gigantic Book of Fishing Stories (2007)

I watched the line grow fatter on the reel. I had watched it run out five times and had lost my heart each time. Now I was gaining on him, and I could feel he was tired.

　　　　　　　　　—Lorian Hemingway, "The Young Woman
and the Sea," *Uncommon Waters* (1991)

Ways to Do It

Night fishing in those lower meadows below the cemetery were filled with delicious shivers of fear. There was swamp fire sometimes in the marl bog downstream, and moonlight danced and gleamed on the polished headstones.

—Ernest G. Schwiebert, Jr., "Memories of Michigan"

. . . the thrill of the blitz never diminishes for the surfcaster.

—Al Ristori, *The Complete Book of Surf Fishing* (2008)

. . . the excitement of a really good night's eel fishing is worthy of compare . . . with the satisfaction derived from howsoever good a day's angling.

—J. H. Keene, *The Practical Fisherman* (1881)

. . . it's hard to beat the thrill of a blue fish blasting a popping plug.

—Al Ristori, *The Complete Book of Surf Fishing* (2008)

Surf fishing is a solitary pursuit.
—Al Ristori, *The Complete Book of Surf Fishing* (2008)

Fishing at night still holds a teenage excitement for me, a keyed-up anticipation of the unpredictable rendezvous waiting out there somewhere in the dark.
—Ian Frazier, *The Fish's Eye: Essays about Angling and the Outdoors* (2002)

Each salmon angler needs to develop a deeper understanding of the fish and the intriguing angling problems involved. . . . Then his last salmon can give him as much pride, satisfaction, and wonder as his first.
—Lee Wulff, Foreword to *The Atlantic Salmon* (1983)

We all tend to fall into angling ruts from time to time, and branching out to search for new species, or try something completely different, can refresh our fishing perspective in a way.
—John Brownlee, "Change of Pace," *Saltwater Sportsman* (February 9, 2012)

Ways to Do It

I personally don't noodle, but I would defend to the death your right to do so.

—Texas State Senator Bob Douell

To the uninitiated, surf fishing looks like a terribly inefficient way to catch fish. It is.

—Barry Stringfellow, "Strange Allure of Surf Fishing," *Yankee Magazine* (July/August 2007)

To fish for Atlantic salmon is to accept a difficult challenge; to capture one, barring an extremely unlucky circumstance, certifies the ability to handle competently our most difficult fishing tackle.

—Lee Wulff, Foreword to *The Atlantic Salmon* (1958)

All fish are not caught with flies.

—John Lyly, *Euphues* (1578)

Ice-fishing isn't so much a sport as it is a way of positively dealing with unfortunate reality.

—John Gierach, *The View from Rat Lake* (1988)

I always strive to discover at least ten things I hadn't known before. They might involve fish behavior, a new lure presentation or knot. Often they center on learning a new lake.
   —Kurt Beckstrom, "Fishing Resolutions for 2012,"
      North American Fisherman (December 30, 2011)

On the blue tin plate in my lap lay a lake-trout filet that was all I had to show from six hours of fishing through a hole cut in two feet of ice. The temperature outside was zero, our warmest night yet by a good ten degrees. This was a hard-earned meal.
   —Gustave Alexson, "Fresh Fish, Frozen Angler," *The New York Times* (March 11, 2010)

Ice fishing does offer a maximum of exercise and labor for a minimum of pleasure and excitement.
   —Arthur R. Macdougall, Jr., "Fishing through the Ice,"
      The Trout Fisherman's Bedside Book (1963)

Ways to Do It

But if you do go ice fishing, do not blame me when you get home, if you do get home. . . . I think that the only important truth I have left out is that a man gets fed up with being comfortable and sane.
—Arthur R. Macdougall, Jr., "Fishing through the Ice,"
The Trout Fisherman's Bedside Book (1963)

I threw a pronounced curve cast and this time when I imparted the minute twitch to the line, the fly moved a sudden inch straight upstream. Then, as it dropped back into a dead drift, it disappeared into the mouth of the best trout of the evening.
—Leonard M. Wright, Jr., *Fishing the Dry Fly as a Living Insect* (1972)

And another thing that makes it easier to ice fish is that one need not worry about his backcasts.
—Arthur R. Macdougall, Jr., "Fishing through the Ice,"
The Trout Fisherman's Bedside Book (1963)

. . . there is no reason whatever why a bottom fisherman cannot enjoy much the same kind of satisfaction as the trout fisherman . . .

—Louis D. Rubin, Jr.,
The Even-Tempered Angler (1983)

If I knew all erbout fishin' fer trout, I wu'd give it up and tackle sunthin' more int'resting.
    —Dud Dean, via Arthur R. Macdougall, Jr. (c. 1949)

I've come to realize all fishing is bait fishing.
    —John Holt, "Death on the Musselshell," *On Killing: Meditations on the Chase* by Robert F. Jones (2001)

It is impossible to lay down inflexible rules for stream fishing.

—Fred Mather

Ways to Do It

Many surveys reveal that 10 percent of fly fishermen catch 90 percent of the fish, and I endorse this finding.
—Lefty Kreh, *Lefty Kreh's Ultimate Guide to Fly Fishing: Everything Anglers Need to Know* (2003)

As an art form, bottom fishing is practiced more often, by more fishermen, than any other kind of sport fishing except that with cane pole and bobber.
—Louis D. Rubin, Jr., *The Even-Tempered Angler* (1983)

I can hear the sound of a trout feeding the same way a mother hears the cough of her child three rooms away.
—Peter Kaminsky, *The Fly Fisherman's Guide to the Meaning of Life* (2008)

Cod fishing: ". . . the men stand on the pitching deck, heavy fishing rods in their hands, dangling clam-baited hooks on the bottom some 150 feet or so below."
—Albert C. Jensen, *The Cod* (1971)

I had caught two fish, one oar, one nose and one jacket sleeve.
—Lewis-Ann Garner, "One for the Glass Case," *Uncommon Waters* (1991)

Ice fishing isn't much of an athletic event.
—Greg Breining, "Wintertime, and Fishing is Easy," *The New York Times* (February 15, 2008)

Ways to Do It

As my state of mind ices over, "ice fishing" becomes redundant—noun and verb freezing over together in suspended animation.
> —Joan Ackermann, "Ice Fishing" (1998)

Hours go by. The drips from my nose freeze up.
> —Joan Ackermann, "Ice Fishing" (1998)

The fish suddenly slips up through the hole, thrashing and thwacking its tail, doubly shocked by its own birth into a waterless world and by its own gasping death.
> —Joan Ackermann, "Ice Fishing" (1998)

WHEN AND WHERE WE
FISH

A wise man once said that the best time to fish is when you can. But that's the busy person's answer and one must add that such factors as the season, time of day, time of tides and hatches, and of course where one fishes will offer clues as to the best times for catching fish. Here again, theories collide—and they certainly are affected by the specific environment and water conditions where you fish. The passionate angler (about whom more later) will always fish when he can and not only make the best of what he finds but enjoy being away from some other, and less pleasant, part of his life. He must simply be content to catch fewer fish—and probably will.

When and Where We Fish

. . . whoever wishes to practice the sport of angling, he must rise early . . .

—Dame Juliana Berners

. . . fish will be found to bite better, always, when conditions are such as to favor the screening of the angler from their ever-watchful eyes, and, when, at the same time, the water is sufficiently clear to enable them to discern the bait on or near the surface.

—Dr. James A. Henshall, *Book of the Black Bass* (1881)

. . . everyone concedes that the fish will not bite in the presence of the public, including newspapermen.

—President Herbert Hoover

I fish all the time when I'm at home; so when I get a chance to go on vacation, I make sure I get in plenty of fishing.

—Thomas McGuane, "Fishing the Big Hole," *An Outside Chance* (1990)

. . . the pleasantest days for the angler's comfort were usually the most propitious and successful days for angling.

—Dr. James A. Henshall,
Book of the Black Bass (1881)

Many of us probably would be better fishermen if we did not spend so much time watching and waiting for the world to become perfect.

—Norman Maclean

The trout do not rise in the cemetery, so you better do your fishing while you are still able.

—Sparse Grey Hackle

A fisherman is good in proportion to the satisfaction he gets out of his sport. [So] a merry duffer is better than a dour master.

—Roderick L. Haig-Brown

When and Where We Fish

. . . all waters are good if they have fish in them.

—Sid W. Gordon

First light is the time when the sky lightens in anticipation of sunrise. It is the best time of day to go fishing for many different kinds of fish.

—Bill Lambot

Overwhelmingly, the reason why so many experienced and well-equipped fishermen catch so few trout is that most of the time they aren't fishing over fish.

—Sparse Grey Hackle, "The Perfect Angler," *Fishless Days, Angling Nights* (1971)

On a bluebird day, sight fishing to twenty-five-pound reds in three feet of clear water was hard to beat.

—Robert Cunningham, *Chasing Records: An Angler's Quest* (2012)

A full moon and a big spangle of stars make a romantic setting, but bass like darkness better. . . . The best fishing usually starts after midnight.
    —H. G. Tapply, *The Sportsman's Notebook* (1964)

It was a long time since Nick had looked into a stream and seen trout. They were very satisfactory.
    —Ernest Hemingway, "Big Two-Hearted River,"
        In Our Time (1925)

To me heaven would be a big bull ring with me holding two barrera seats and a trout stream outside that no one else was allowed to fish in . . .
                    —Ernest Hemingway

In the recollection of the trout fisherman it is always spring. The blackbird sings of a May morning. The little trout jump in the riffles, and the German brown comes surely to the fly on the evening rise.
    —R. Palmer Baker, Jr., *The Sweet of the Year* (1965)

When and Where We Fish

Every year or so a new gimmick on fish feeding times
hits the market . . . anglers are every bit as gullible as
dieters.
> —Leonard M. Wright, Jr., *The Ways of Trout* (1985)

At the commencement of the open season, and until
the young maple are half grown, bait will be found
more successful than the fly.
> —George W. Sears (Nessmuk)

Nick did not like to fish with other men on the river.
Unless they were of your party, they spoiled it.
> —Ernest Hemingway, "Big Two-Hearted River,"
> *In Our Time* (1925)

There is time to go long, time to go short and time to
go fishing.
> —Jesse Livermore, quoted in *Come Into My Trading
> Room* by Alexander Elder (2002)

155

[Y]ou'll get to the point where you won't want to take a vacation unless fishing is involved.
—N. Macauley Lord, "Casting a Line, Catching Yourself," *The New York Times*, written by Deidre Fanning (June 7, 2002)

On my trip to Argentina, I learned that fly fishing is an international language.
—Rabbi Eric Eisenkramer, "Fly Fishing in Argentina," *The Fly Fishing Rabbi* (January 5, 2008)

In bass fishing we have thought the moon to be an advantage. If it does not guide the prey to the lure, it at least lends beauty to the scene and bathes in its pale light the surroundings of the fisherman, which are often so exceedingly beautiful.

—Seth Green

When and Where We Fish

May Easter find us at the trysting-place, there where the dancing bubbles spin and race, to meet the first March Brown!
>—Patrick R. Chalmers, "To An Old Friend,"
>*Green Days and Blue Days* (1914)

Is this the perfect fly for the water temperature, the insect activity, the time of year? Answer: Yes. This morning, in the brightening Vermont sunlight, I am making fly fishing mine.
>—Allison Moir, "Love the Man, Love the Fly Rod," *A Different Angle: Fly Fishing Stories by Women* (1995)

We fished a good deal, but we did not average one fish a week. We could see trout by the thousand winging about in the emptiness under us, or sleeping in shoals on the bottom, but they would not bite.
>—Mark Twain, *Roughing It* (1872)

A true surf-caster is a man who loves the sea. Far beyond the prize of any great fish he might land is the exhilaration of the wave.
—Negley Farson, *Going Fishing* (1943)

Tide is a critical factor when fishing the surf as even small changes in water level can make all the difference.
—Al Ristori, *The Complete Book of Surf Fishing* (2008)

Fishing always reaches its peak at a time when the bugs are thickest. And bugs are thickest at the places where fishing is best. . . . So whenever and wherever you enjoy good fishing you can expect to find mosquitoes, black flies, midges, or deerflies, all lusting for your life's blood.
—H. G. Tapply, *The Sportsman's Notebook* (1964)

When and Where We Fish

. . . the best fishing during mayfly hatches is definitely
on days when the weather is poor.

> —John Juracek and Craig Mathews

The two best times to fish is when it's rainin' and
when it ain't.

> —Patrick F. McManus

Nothing says "fish me" like a smallmouth river in July.

> —Will Ryan, "Rivers of Bronze,"
> *Field & Stream* (July 2005)

There is . . . one constant in all types of fishing, which
is: The time the fish are biting is almost but not quite
now.

> —P. J. O'Rourke, "A Fly Fishing Primer,"
> *Sports Illustrated* (July 31, 1989)

ESPECIALLY FOR FLY FISHERS

Not everyone with a passion for fishing becomes a fly fisher. But a lot do. It is sufficiently different from all other forms of angling that it has developed a full subculture with its own concerns and even its own language.

Admittedly, fly fishing seems to demand more of its practitioners—knowledge of entomology, perhaps, of fly patterns and the construction of those little feathered lures that mostly imitate bugs; it concerns itself with casting techniques more than bait casting or spinning; it often demands different ways of approaching and fighting fish in fresh and salt water, and much else that you will discover in this section.

Fly fishing also creates its own special brand of snob—the person who thinks himself superior because he fly fishes at all, or he who uses only flies that float. What silliness—like the notion that a fly fisher is a "he" to begin with.

Especially for Fly Fishers

But I have found fly fishing endlessly engaging, endlessly demanding, and prefer it simply because its challenges give me the most satisfaction, even when it frustrates my best efforts.

No sport affords a greater field for observation and study than fly fishing, and it is the close attention paid to the minor happenings upon the stream that marks the finished angler.

—George M. L. La Branche,
The Dry Fly and Fast Water (1914)

When you are next complaining about the selectivity of trout, bear the thought in mind: Were it not for this fortunate trait, how long would our stream fishing last?
—Art Flick, *Art Flick's Streamside Guide to Naturals and their Limitations* (1947)

I do not know anything more beautiful in nature than the head-and-tailing trout.

—Harry Plunket-Green,
Where the Bright Waters Meet (1936)

Especially for Fly Fishers

To be consistently successful in his pursuit of the
various gamefishes, the all-around fly angler must
be at least amateur entomologist, ichthyologist, and
meteorologist.

—Tom McNally,
The Complete Book of Fly Fishing (1993)

Fly fishing . . . requires an intimacy with bugs, birds,
weather, water and fish that sticking a worm on a hook
never asked of me.

—Ailm Travler, "Fly Fishing Folly,"
Uncommon Waters (1991)

A fly fisherman's knowledge is compounded of many
things. It grows out of imagination, curiosity, bold
experiment, and intense obvservation.

—Roderick L. Haig-Brown,
A River Never Sleeps (1946)

A spin fisherman can fish a river; a fly fisherman must know a river.

—Dave Hughes

He told us about Christ's disciples being fishermen, and we were left to assume . . . that all great fishermen on the Sea of Galilee were fly fishermen and that John, the favorite, was a dry-fly fisherman.
—Norman Maclean, *A River Runs through It* (1976)

Certainly no aspect of fly fishing is as enjoyable as those which have a good, firmly based and well-established myth or two for company.

—Conrad Voss Bark

To the experimental and inquiring mind, casting a fly onto the stream is one part of a never-ending study of nature.
—John Atherton, *The Fly and the Fish* (1951)

Especially for Fly Fishers

[Fly fishing] is like any other skill, whether it's the knowledge of the Roy Lopez opening in chess, how to hit a golf ball straight, or put spin on a tennis ball, the sheer pleasure of doing something difficult well.

—Conrad Voss Bark, *A Fly on the Water* (1986)

The lessons that fly fishing delivers will come whether you're in sweet water or salt water. All the fish are interesting . . .

—Bill Lambot

In fly fishing, compromises are often perfectly acceptable; there are few absolutes. I guess you could say the same thing about marriage.

—Ken Marsh, *Alaska Magazine*

Once the fly is tied onto the tippet of my leader, it is more than an imitation insect, it is my guide into another world.

—Ailm Travler, "Fly Fishing Folly,"
Uncommon Waters (1991)

The Edwards fly rod in my hand connected me to a universe of meanings.
—George Black, *Casting a Spell: The Bamboo Fly Rod and the American Pursuit of Perfection* (2006)

Perhaps any angler is driven by voodoo entymology; but one thing is certain: Successful fly fishing will always somehow elude sheer willpower.
—Thomas McGuane, Foreword to *Spring Creeks* by Mike Lawson (2003)

Especially for Fly Fishers

Nymph fishing, new certainly in its modern dress, but in essence as old as fly-fishing itself.

—John Waller Hills, *River Keeper: The Life of William James Lunn* (1934)

Skill at the riverside, or at the fly-table, never came, nor ever will come to us by any road than that of practice.

—George M. Kelson, *The Salmon Fly* (1895)

. . . if you catch nothing, fly-casting is, like virtue, its own exceedingly great reward.

—Fred Mather, *My Angling Friends* (1901)

. . . wild trout will take almost any fly and the educated trout will take only those that imitate in color and action their natural food as they see it.

—Lee Wulff

The indications which tell your dry-fly angler when to strike are clear and unmistakable, but those which bid a wet-fly man raise his rod-point and draw in the steel are frequently so subtle, so evanescent and impalpable to the senses, that, when the bending rod assures him that he has divined aright, he feels an ecstasy as though he had performed a miracle each time.

—G. E. M. Skues,
Minor Tactics of the Chalk Stream (1910)

Never forget: Fly fishing is fun partly *because* it is frustrating.

—Phil Monahan, "The Agony and the Ecstasy,"
Orvisnews.com (April 2, 2012)

I have tried expressionist flies—but they work only on expressionist fish, like bass . . .

—Le Anne Schreiber

Especially for Fly Fishers

. . . we should take an interest in insects because they are, after all, the root of our sport. Without them there is no basis for fly fishing.

—John Juracek and Craig Mathews,
Fishing Yellowstone Hatches (1992)

The best imitations can scarcely be pronounced good until tested by the fish.

—Michael Theakston

There is no fly-fishing circumstance where casting poorly will offer an advantage.

—Tom Rosebauer,
The Orvis Guide to Beginning Fly Fishing (2009)

. . . the fact is indisputable that the shabbiest, most dilapidated, most broken-winged fly is as likely to kill as the newest and freshest of the fly-tier's confections—provided size and color be right.

—G. E. M. Skues, *The Way of a Trout with a Fly* (1921)

1,001 Pearls of Fishing Wisdom

The truth is, fly fishing is folly: useless, unreasonable, irrational, and without purpose.
—Ailm Travler, "Fly Fishing Folly,"
Uncommon Waters (1991)

If I'm not going to catch anything, then I'd rather not catch anything on flies.
—Bob Lawless

. . . neither time nor repetition has destroyed the illusion that the rise of a trout to a dry fly is properly regarded in the light of a miracle.
—Harold F. Blaisdell,
The Philosophical Fisherman (1969)

Just as in cooking there's no such thing as a little garlic, in fishing there's no such thing as a little drag.
—H. G. Tapply, *The Sportsman's Notebook* (1964)

Especially for Fly Fishers

Fly fishing is to fishing as ballet is to walking.
—Howell Raines, *Fly Fishing through the Midlife Crisis* (1993)

Fly-fishing is the most fun you can have standing up.
—Arnold Gingrich

I ain't got no objection to them fellers with the jinted poles. And I don't mind nuther their standin' off and throwin' their flies as far as they've a mind to. But what does rile me is the cheeky way in which they stand up and say there isn't no decent way of fishin' but their way.
—Frank R. Stockton

Fly-fishers fail in preparing their bait so as to make it alluring in the right quarter, for want of a due acquaintance with the subjectivity of fishes.
—George Eliot, *The Mill on the Floss* (1860)

Cast your fly with confidence.

—Theodore Gordon

. . . there are enough miles of bright water in the Blue Ridge to support the fly fisherman's deep-seated need to believe in infinite possibilities.

—Christopher Camuto,
A Fly Fisherman's Blue Ridge (1990)

The game [of nods] is played by tying a reasonable facsimile of the insect being taken by the trout. Then many variations of this basic pattern are tied with only slight differences in each of them. These are in turn cast to a visible feeding trout, and his reaction noted very carefully. . . . Each fly is cast as long as it receives a nod from the trout. When it no longer excites any nods it is discarded for a new variation.

—Vincent C. Marinaro, *In the Ring of the Rise* (1976)

Especially for Fly Fishers

. . . knowing a river intimately is a very large part of the joy of fly fishing.

—Roderick L. Haig-Brown,
A River Never Sleeps (1946)

. . . the dry fly magician, the man who can, with seven ounces of split cane, send a "Tup's indispensible" at the end of four yards of ax gut anywhere, to do, in all conditions, any jiggery-pokery round-the-corner job required of it, is the best of all . . .

—Patrick R. Chalmers, *At the Tail of the Weir* (1932)

No wonder, then, that the fly fisher loves at times to take a day all by himself; for his very loneliness begets a comfortable feeling of independence and leisure, and a quiet assurance of resources within himself to meet all difficulties that may arise.

—Thaddeus Norris,
The American Angler's Book (1864)

No form of fishing offers such elaborate silences as fly-fishing for permit.
—Thomas McGuane, *The Longest Silence* (1999)

Order of Why Trout Take
The light-effects of the fly, above and below the surface
The way the fly is cast and manipulated, including where the fly is placed relative to the fish
Visibility of the leader to the fish
The size of the fly
Design of the fly
Color of the fly
Accuracy of imitation of natural insects
—Edward R. Hewitt, *A Trout and Salmon Fisherman for Seventy-Five Years* (1948)

Especially for Fly Fishers

Learn to identify, and to fish with, the "fly on the water." But do it for the plain, commonsense reason that you are thereby quadrupling your pleasure (to say nothing of rather more than doubling your bag) . . .
  —J. W. Dunne, *Sunshine and the Dry Fly* (1924)

Picking up a fly rod and flipping it like a buggy whip tells nothing of its quality.

         —Sid W. Gordon

To go through an entire angling life without consciously killing a single fish is a tame, unconscious, disconnected approach to flyfishing . . .
  —John Holt, "Death on the Musselshell," *On Killing: Meditations on the Chase* by Robert F. Jones (2001)

Even after a knowledge of mayflies is attained, things will often work out other than expected.

          —Art Flick

The wonderful obstinacy of the dry-fly purist!
—William Humphrey, *My Moby Dick* (1978)

About the only certainty, other than uncertainty, in fly fishing is that a fly won't catch fish if it stays in its box.
—Arnold Gingrich, *The Joys of Trout* (1973)

Fishing textbooks being written by intensely practical men, sometimes omit to remind us, if their authors think of it at all, that fly fishing needs to have a touch of magic about it if we are to enjoy it to the full.
—Conrad Voss Bark, *A Fly on the Water* (1986)

. . . when you're flyfishing in a run you should at least own the remainder of the run below you.
—Austin McPherson, "The Gorge," *Fly Rod & Reel Online* (October 29, 2008)

Especially for Fly Fishers

That one does not fish for trout with spinning lures or live bait is taken for granted, along with toilet training.
—William Humphrey

. . . this winter I rounded up all the various, multihued and textured nymphs I had ever tied and put them in a box marked "nymphs." I decided I didn't want to fish nymphs anymore. Just like that.
—Ailm Travler, "Run-Off," *A Different Angle: Fly Fishing Stories by Women* (1995)

Spring creek trout have a reputation for being moody, which often means they are difficult, but when they're in the mood to feast, almost nothing—not sloppy wading, not poor casting, not a ridiculous choice of flies—will dissuade them.
—Ted Leeson, *Jerusalem Creek* (2002)

We wish to reproduce as nearly as possibly the effect of insects as it floats upon the stream; to deceive the trout that have had enough experience of flies and of fishermen to make them a bit shy and crafty.

—Theodore Gordon

More than half the time, a trout will refuse your fly not because the fly was wrong but because it was not behaving properly.

—Tom Rosenbauer, *The Orvis Guide to Beginning Fly Fishing* (2009)

When getting skunked for hours, I try to rationalize the situation, saying: "I'll just use this time to practice my casting." That usually does not work for long. The sport is called fly fishing, not fly casting.

—Rabbi Eric Eisenkramer, "Fly Fishing and Frustration," *The Fly Fishing Rabbi* (January 17, 2011)

Especially for Fly Fishers

Sometimes the essence of a fly may be only a touch of color, perhaps orange with a touch of blue flash. That's it. A detail that is also the core. What can you do with something as vague as that? A great deal.

—Ken Abrames, *The Perfect Fish;
Illusions in Fly Tying* (1999)

The number of ways in which flies can be tied is incredible. There are hardly two books which lay down identical methods.

—G. E. M. Skues, *The Way of a Trout with a Fly* (1921)

Fly fishing is about adaptation—in any role, capacity, or genre.

—Charles Jardine, Foreword to *Dynamic Nymphing:
Tactics, Techniques, and Flies from Around the World*
by George Daniel (2012)

The trout fly will not only survive the times, but will assuredly continue its evolution as it has done for nigh on five-hundred years. In all that time, neither trout nor the delicate insects . . . have changed. Only man and his ideas are changing . . .

—W. H. Lawrie, *A Reference Book of English Trout Flies* (1967)

Why, to anchor you with what paltry knowledge the two of us have of fly fishing, would make as much sense as a second-rate con man trying to teach his kids the ropes, the same crap that put the old man in the slammer in the first place.

—Harry Middleton's grandfather, Emerson, *The Earth is Enough: Growing Up in a World of Flyfishing, Trout & Old Men* (1989)

Especially for Fly Fishers

"Invention" is a fragile concept in fly fishing. Hardly any idea is completely new . . . it might be a more important thing to refine an old invention so successfully that the world notices.

—Paul Schullery, "A Dreadful Scourge," *American Angler* (December 8, 2010)

In the lexicon of the fly-fisherman, the words "rise" and "hooked" connote the successful and desirable climax; landing a fish is purely anticlimax.

—Vincent C. Marinaro

Time flies so fast after youth is past that we cannot accomplish one half the many things we have in mind or indeed one half our duties. The only safe and sensible plan is to make other things give way to the essentials, and the first of these is fly fishing.

—Theodore Gordon

Often, I have been exhausted on trout streams, uncomfortable, wet, cold, briar scarred, sunburned, mosquito bitten, but never, with a fly rod in my hand, have I been in a place that was less than beautiful.

—Charles Kuralt

The reason that all other kinds of fishermen look up to the dry-fly purist is not that he catches more fish than they; on the contrary, it is because he catches fewer. His is the sport in its purest, most impractical, least material form.

—William Humphrey

Fly-fishing may well be considered the most beautiful of all rural sports.

—W. H. Herbert (Frank Forester)

Especially for Fly Fishers

Tail fins, snouts poking out of weedbeds, silver patches where scales are missing against gravels, pinky warts. The more exacting flyfisher looks into the river and asks himself, "When is a trout not a trout?" He looks for imaginary trout and takes away the tail, the fins, the gills, the body, the head—hoping something in the tight area he scans holds one or more elements of a trout. Only then can he conclude that a trout is not a trout—when it was never there in the first place.

—Neil Patterson, *Chalkstream Chronicle* (1995)

Fly fishermen are generally well camouflaged. Indeed, some are so well camouflaged that a senior member of the Flyfishers' who fished the Kennet at Chamberhouse had the reputation of being practically indistinguishable from a tree.

—Conrad Voss Bark, *A Fly on the Water* (1986)

Now and then fishermen get excited about a fly that has been "outlawed" in England or the Sahara Desert. That fly is said to be a wicked killer.
—Arthur R. Macdougall, Jr., "The Best Fly Is Not Yet," *The Trout Fisherman's Bedside Book* (1963)

. . . fly tying is the next best thing to fishing; it is the sort of licking of the lips that eases a thirsty man in the desert.
—Arthur Ransome, "Fly Tying in Winter," *Rod and Line* (1929)

The trout fly of today grew out of the trout fly of yesterday.
—John McDonald, Introduction to *The Complete Fly Fisherman* (1947)

Especially for Fly Fishers

A man can be a fish hog with a fly rod as easily as he
can with a cane pole. Easier perhaps.
—H. G. Tapply, *The Sportsman's Notebook* (1964)

Any meticulous attention to color or detail [in a fly
pattern] is wasted effort.
—Vincent C. Marinaro, *In the Ring of the Rise* (1976)

There is only one secret in dry-fly fishing, which is to
make an artificial fly float over a trout in such a way
that it looks appetizing enough for him to swallow.
—Dermot Wilson, *Fishing the Dry Fly* (1970)

For this form of fishing [with a wet fly], the rod is no longer a shooting machine but a receiving post, with super-sensitive antennae, capable of registering immediately the slightest reaction of the fish to the fly.
—Charles Ritz, *A Fly Fisher's Life* (1959)

Fly-fishing may be a very pleasant amusement; but angling, or float-fishing, I can only compare to a stick and a string, with a worm at one end and a fool at the other.

—Dr. Samuel Johnson

Especially for Fly Fishers

. . . there are times when flyfishing can seem
childishly easy.
   —Tom Sutcliffe, MD, *Reflections on Flyfishing* (1990)

It is the constant—or inconstant—change, the infinite
variety in fly-fishing that binds us fast. It is impossible
to grow weary of a sport that is never the same on
any two days of the year.

                                        —Theodore Gordon

BIG FISH

A truly big bluegill might reach two pounds and a monster rainbow trout might weigh five pounds in some waters or twenty in others. There is a certain amount of relativity when speaking of big fish. I have seen a few trout in small, clear streams that set my heart racing and yet they were no larger than blue-runners used as bait for thousand-pound marlin. Still, all anglers are involved with big fish whether that fish is a king of its species or of the place it inhabits or of all species. Some anglers want the biggest quarry for the prestige, for the trophy, for the satisfaction of size. It's certainly true that a great fish adds a certain mysterious and exciting quality to whatever water it inhabits—and fishing in waters that hold such giants is tremendously exciting for many who fish. I've caught a few of these prodigies of nature—usually by chance—and lost even more, and the ones I lost have brought even more memories than one would if stuffed and decorating my wall.

Big Fish

Adieu, O trout of marvelous size,
Thou piscatorial speckled wonder.
—George W. Sears (Nessmuk)

When the fish took the lure, he did not explode in a
geyser of white water. He did not rocket out of the
water like a twelve-inch projectile. He did not erupt, or
detonate, or blast the lure, or attempt any of the other
warlike measures commonly attributed to big fish in
the literature of outdoor magazines. Being intelligent,
if not widely read, he tried to eat the lure.
—Red Smith, "Mucha Trucha," *Great Outdoor Adventures* (1961)

. . . fishing for giant bluefin tuna, those swimming
Volkswagons weighing nearly a thousand pounds
each.
—Albia Dugger, "The Search for the Sword," *Uncommon Waters* (1991)

He was a lusty rainbow of twelve pounds with shoulders like Max Baer's, magnificently colored, and splendidly deep, like Jane Russell. I killed him and helped eat him and I am stilled awed by him.
> —Red Smith, "Mucha Trucha," *Great Outdoor Adventures* (1961)

The fact is that the fly fisherman is likely to raise his biggest and most difficult trout when he is on the stream alone, concentrating and undisturbed.
> —R. Palmer Baker, Jr.

Big browns . . . take when they feel like it, which isn't often, and they do most of their feeding at night, which is how they get big.
> —Robert M. Mengel

Every man has a fish in his life that haunts him.
> —Negley Farson

Big Fish

Like the fish that haunts the angler's dreams, he was forever gaining size.

—Harry Middleton, *The Earth Is Enough: Growing Up in a World of Flyfishing, Trout & Old Men* (1989)

Lord give me strength to catch a fish. So big, that even I, when speaking of it to my friends, may never need to lie.

—Anonymous

Find the baitfish first and then you'll usually locate the bigger fish too.

—Vlad Evanoff, *2002 Fishing Tips and Tricks* (1999)

Out of the water he came, all twelve pounds of him, bright and beautiful. And I fell in love again.

—Joan Wulff, "Where I Want to Be"

When a plump two-pound trout refuses to eat a tinseled feathered fraud, I am not the man to refuse him something more edible.

—George W. Sears (Nessmuk)

I daresay my friend could cast a fly like an angel, if he put his hand to it; but his mind was on size, nothing else. Huge fish peered at you from every wall of his fine house in London. Dinner conversation was about nothing else. He *was* a fanatic fisherman, so touchy about it that when I tried to rag him that sunset— asking what four flies he had brought up—the beer itself seemed to become soured by his resentment.

—Negley Farson, *Going Fishing* (1943)

I unhesitatingly assert that there is no single moment with horse or gun into which is concentrated such a thrill of hope, fear, expectation, and exultation as that of the rise and successful striking of a heavy salmon.

—H. Cholmondeley-Pennell

Big Fish

The fish and I were both stunned and disbelieving to find ourselves connected by a line.

—William Humphrey

. . . even in faster water, the bigger fish dominates the feeding stations where a better look is possible: the long seams, the well-defined riffle corners with the isometrics of current well spaced, the luxury apartments of steambed hydrology.

—Thomas McGuane, *The Longest Silence* (1999)

If you catch a big fish from a certain spot keep that location in your mind. Sooner or later, another big fish will move in to take its place.

—Vlad Evanoff, *2002 Fishing Tips and Tricks* (1999)

Big fish, lots of them, all the time has become a contemporary motto.

—Ted Leeson, Foreword to *The Fly Fisher's Craft: The Art and History* by Darrel Martin (2006)

Nothing makes a fish bigger than almost being caught.
—Author Unknown

I've experienced very little in life as defeating as losing a big fish.

—Jake Mosher

For, as it is often the case with trout, the big ones are very quiet risers.

—Francis Francis

For an instant there was a flash of light in the darkness of the depths, not the brown of shark or the gold of tuna, but the pure silver-blue of swordfish gleaming in the crystal Yucatan depths.
—Albia Dugger, "The Search for the Sword," *Uncommon Waters* (1991)

Big Fish

. . . more big fish are caught within a range of fifteen
yards than outside it . . .
—Dermot Wilson, *Fishing the Dry Fly* (1970)

I never lost a little fish—
Yes, I am free to say.
It always was the biggest fish
I caught, that got away.

—Eugene Field

If you catch a large bass in midsummer, assume it's
part of a school of similar-size fish.
—Jerome B. Robinson, "Jerry's Tips,"
Field & Stream (July 2005)

I well remember the first big fish that succumbed to
my wriggling worm. He was a roach all of six inches in
length.
—John Goddard, *John Goddard's Trout Fishing
Techniques: Practical Fly Fishing Solutions* (1996)

. . . the big fish, yellow looking in the water, swimming two or three feet under the surface, the huge pectoral fins tucked close to the flanks, the dorsal fin down, the fish looking a round fast-moving log in the water except for the erect curve of that slicing tail.

—Ernest Hemingway, "Marlin off the Morro: A Cuban Letter," *Esquire* (Autumn 1933)

There are plenty of tuna and they take the bait. It is a back-sickening, sinew-straining, man-sized job even with a rod that looks like a hoe handle.

—Ernest Hemingway, "Tuna Fishing in Spain," *Toronto Star Weekly* (February 18, 1922)

Every day I see the head of the largest trout I ever hooked, but did not land.

—Theodore Gordon

Big Fish

It seems that worms had somehow gotten a bad name. I think a fishing pal of mine hit it on the head when he said, "It just pisses them off that you can catch trout, I mean really big trout, on a fly that a five-year-old can tie in twenty seconds!"

—Ed Engle, *Fly Fishing the Tailwaters* (1991)

Two times I turned the fish. He took to the air. A monster! I pulled his head up one more time and had him pointed toward open water when he bore down on a log, wrapped me and was off!

—Peter Kaminsky, "Trout Fresh from the Sea at the End of the Earth in Argentina," *The New York Times* (May 20, 2009)

. . . no man who has ever lost a truly noteworthy fish has ever forgotten it.

—Arnold Gingrich, *The Joys of Trout* (1973)

I doubt if I shall ever outgrow the excitement bordering on panic which I feel the instant I know I have a strong unmanageable fish, be it brook trout, brown trout, cutthroat, steelhead, or salmon on my line.

—Edward Weeks, *Fresh Waters* (1968)

The existence of such omniscient giants as he, sentient in the deeps of a great pool, gives glamour to a stream and to all the fishing upon it.

—Howard T. Walden II, *Upstream and Down* (1938)

It's a thrill to hook a big fish in a small boat.

—Dave DiBenedetto, as quoted by Wendy Knight in "A Tippy Test for Anglers: Landing Fish from a Kayak," *The New York Times* (September 9, 2005)

Big Fish

We struggled with one another, back and forth along the bank, until I landed it, gills heaving, in the sand.
　　　　　—Nancy Lord, "Magadan Luck," *Uncommon Waters* (1991)

I like to keep a big fish as calm and quiet as possible and lick him by nagging him to death a little at a time.
　　　　　—Vincent C. Marinaro, "The Hidden Hatch," *In the Ring of the Rise* (1976)

He had been hooked two or three times and was consequently as wary as a miser, when his son begins to beat about the bush, introductory to some pecuniary hint.
　　　　　—Hewitt Wheatly, *The Rod and Line* (1849)

Truly large trout rarely move far for a single insect.
—Dave Hughes, *Reading the Water: A Fly Fisher's Handbook for Finding Trout in All Types of Water* (1988)

The odds of catching a trophy-class fish are inversely proportional to how much you deserve to catch one.
—Larry Dahlberg, "Dahlberg's Law of Fishing"

Big Fish

Now I am . . . like anyone with a strong preference for the fly rod, totally indifferent to how large a fish I catch by comparison with other fishermen. So when a fifteen-year-old called Fred, fishing deep in midsummer with a hideously plastic worm, caught a four and a half pounder . . . I naturally felt no resentment beyond wanting to break the kid's thumbs.

—Vance Bourjaily

ADDICTION,
COMPULSION

Many anglers speak of being "addicted" to fishing. The simplest and most generous translation of what they mean might be, "I like it a lot and fish whenever I can." But in a lot of instances the passion to fish amounts to more of a "compulsion" to do so, perhaps a true addiction, and like all addictions it is best controlled lest it control you. In the world of angling this might be as simple a matter as ending a day with the "one last cast" you speak of rather than taking another hour and fifty more casts. It might mean not buying twenty rods but the two or three you really need. As Sparse Grey Hackle says, "A man can become so caught up in fishing that it actually becomes a grim business"—which sounds like the great joy and fun of it has somehow turned sour.

Addiction, Compulsion

A man can become so caught up in fishing that it actually becomes a grim business . . .
>—Sparse Grey Hackle, "Murder," *Fishless Days, Angling Nights* (1971)

Fishing simply sent me out of my mind. I could neither think nor talk of anything else, so that mother was angry and said that she would not let me fish again because I might fall ill from such excitement.
>—Sergei Aksakov, "Memoir," translated by Arthur Ransome

If, as I suspect, trout fishing is something of a disease, then it is also something of a therapy in itself.
>—Tom Sutcliffe, MD, *Reflections on Fishing* (1990)

The angling fever is a very real disease and can only be cured by the application of cold water and fresh, untainted air.

—Theodore Gordon

There are always greater fish than you have caught, always the lure of greater task and achievement, always the inspiration to seek, to endure, to find.

—Zane Grey

Fishing . . . is conducted under continuous tension.
—Arthur Ransome, "Fisherman's Patience,"
Rod and Line (1929)

Work is for people who don't know how to fish.
—Paul A. Volcker

Addiction, Compulsion

One of the fishers told the crowd he ran a hundred miles or more each day to catch fish. The next day we spotted him fishing near the boat launch.
>—Joe Skorupa, "Big Event, Small Fish,"
>*Popular Mechanics* (December 1987)

Depending upon who's doing the counting, making a perfect bamboo fly rod involves anything from thirty to a hundred steps—even a thousand . . .
>—George Black, *Casting a Spell: The Bamboo Fly Rod and the American Pursuit of Perfection* (2006)

Perhaps the reason I have brought so eager a passion to the fishing of so many rivers is that I have never had enough of it.
>—Ferris Greenslet, *Under the Bridge* (1943)

A Voss Bark Trio
An elderly member of a distinguished fishing club . . .
became so bored during the winter closed season that
he used to take his fly boxes to bed.
The wife, plucking an errant Blue Charm from a
sensitive part of her anatomy, possibly in the dead of
night, had a legitimate complaint.
His wife, a good woman at heart, allowed him back
into her bed, with his boxes, providing he counted his
flies before and after.
>   —Conrad Voss Bark, *A Fly on the Water* (1986)

I became known around town as "the-kid-who-is-the-
nut-on-fishing" . . .
>   —Jean Shepherd, "Hairy Gertz and the Forty-Seven
> Crappies," *In God We Trust, All Others Pay Cash* (1966)

Addiction, Compulsion

After the doctor's departure Koznyshev expressed the
wish to go to the river with his fishing rod. He was
fond of angling and was apparently proud of being
fond of such a stupid occupation.
> —Leo Tolstoy, *Anna Karenina* (1877)

Everyone ought to believe in something; I believe I'll
go fishing.

> —Anonymous

[Some bamboo fly-rod makers] were driven to poverty,
divorce, or the brink of madness by the demands they
placed upon themselves.
> —George Black, *Casting a Spell: The Bamboo Fly Rod
> and the American Pursuit of Perfection* (2006)

1,001 Pearls of Fishing Wisdom

The awkward fisherman does nothing but disturb the water.

—Anonymous

The feeling about fishing is a lot like that about sex, that of course it's better when it's good, but it's not bad when it isn't.

—Arnold Gingrich, *The Joys of Trout* (1973)

Fly fishing for trout has wrecked men's marriages, their careers; when begun early enough in life it has prevented them from ever getting around to either marriage or career and turned them into lifelong celibates and ne'er-do-wells.

—William Humphrey, *My Moby Dick* (1978)

[Next year] I will leave the river when I promise my wife I will leave.

—Brian Clarke

Addiction, Compulsion

Here lies poor Thompson, all alone,
As dead and cold as any stone.
In wading in the river Nith,
He took a cold, which stopp'd his breath.
He fish'd the stream for ten years past,
Death caught him in his net at last.

> —Written on a tombstone in Dumphries,
> England; quoted by Tim Ben in *The (Almost)
> Complete Angler* (1988)

Fish or no fish, whenever opportunity offers, the
angler may be found at the waterside.

> —John Burroughs, *Pepacton* (1881)

There are occasions when ninety-nine trout out of a
hundred will come to net with comparative
ease . . . It is the hundredth trout that fascinates the
serious fly fisher.

> —Brian Clarke and John Goddard,
> *The Trout and the Fly* (1980)

I often hear someone say, "Well, I need to get in that deep to reach the other side." So I ask, "Are all the trout on the other side?"

> —A. K. Best, *Fly Fishing with A. K.* (2005)

Now if we are out fishing together, he stands well back from me; his only other option is to buy shares in a bandage company.

> —Lewis-Ann Garner, "One for the Glass Case," *Uncommon Waters* (1991)

. . . the sporting qualities of a fish are dependent neither on its size nor its weight, but on the effort of concentration, the skill and mastery it demands from the fisherman.

> —Charles Ritz, *A Fly Fisher's Life* (1959)

Addiction, Compulsion

Yet fish there be, that
Neither hook nor line
Nor snare, nor net, nor
Engine can make thine.
> —John Bunyan, *Pilgrim's Progress* (1678)

If fishing interferes with your business, give up your
business . . . the trout do not rise in Greenwood
Cemetery.
> —Sparse Grey Hackle, "Murder," *Fishless Days,*
> *Angling Nights* (1971)

If a little madness be a necessary requisite to obtain
the ultimate in the pleasure of angling—then O Lord,
give me insanity!

> —John Alden Knight

. . . you will search far to find a fisherman to admit that a taste for fishing, like a taste for liquor, must be governed lest it come to possess its possessor; that an excess of fishing can cause as many tragedies of lost purpose, earning power, and position as an excess of liquor.

—Sparse Grey Hackle, *Fishing Days, Angling Nights* (1971)

Catch and Release fishing is a lot like golf. You don't have to eat the ball to have a good time.

—Anonymous

Ice fishing (ís-fish-ing) n. A recreational attempt to catch food/hypothermia.

—Alyssa Giacobbe

Wet boots are a way of life.

—Austin McPherson

Addiction, Compulsion

Are you wishing
Jolly fishing?
This way sir!
I'll teach you.

> —Henry Van Dyke, "The Angler's Reveille,"
> *The Poems of Henry Van Dyke* (1911)

Have you ripped any lips?

> —Mindless query to a fellow angler

In the big pocket way in the back of my vest are a
couple of highly flexible honey and oats granola bars
and a badly misshapen Snickers bar. I have no idea
how long they've been there, but I'll leave them there
just in case.

> —A. K. Best, *Fly Fishing with A. K.* (2005)

I have learned not to go crazy if I hike for a while only
to find someone in my private water.

> —Steven J. Meyers, *San Juan River Chronicle* (1994)

. . . the tyrannical fascination which angling holds
for all those who have once been initiated into its
mysteries.

—Rafael Sabatini

Angling, too, that solitary vice,
Whatever Izaak Walton sings or says;
The quaint, old, cruel coxcomb in his gullet
Should have a hook, and a small trout to pull it.

—Lord Byron, *Don Juan* (1818)

Even eminent chartered accountants are known,
in their capacity as fishermen, blissfully to ignore
differences between seven and ten inches, half a
pound and two pounds, three fish and a dozen fish.

—William Sherwood Fox,
Silken Lines and Silver Hooks (1954)

Addiction, Compulsion

I don't think that harassing fish all day just to feel a tug on my line is such a great idea; as Holly puts it, catch and release is a lot like shooting ducks with a Taser, just to watch them fall. I fish to eat. Period.

—Hank Shaw, "Man, Nature, and Trout: Our Vanishing Traditions," *The Atlantic* (April 12, 2011)

A really crushing blow from Fate, such as the loss of three salmon one after the other . . .

—H. T. Sheringham, *Fishing: Its Cause, Treatment, and Cure* (c. 1912)

S: Folks will go to any lengths to catch fish, won't they?
F: Well, yes, Aristotle says that the balletomane skate can easily be caught by a pair of fishermen, using a net if one plays music and the other dances on the deck.

—John Hersey, *Blues* (1987)

It mattered little what the weather was, and scarcely more as to the time of year, John Pike must have his fishing every day, and on Sundays he read about it and made flies. All the rest of the time he was thinking about it.

—R. D. Blackmore, "Crocker's Hole" (1895)

There comes a time in every man's life when he is either going to go fishing or do something worse.
—Havilah Babcock, "When a Lady Undresses" (1947)

Neek, all I want to do is feesh, feesh, feesh. Everywhere. All the time.

—Pierre Affre, *To the author* (c. 1985; also 1998)

Hell, if I'd jumped on all the dames I'm supposed to have jumped on, I'd have had no time to go fishing.

—Clark Gable

Addiction, Compulsion

The flies orbited me at several quantum levels,
chewed my forearms through my shirtsleeve vents,
made inroads under my collar, took long excursions
between T-shirt and skin. . . . I didn't see a single fish.
—Ian Frazier, *The Fish's Eye: Essays about Angling and
the Outdoors* (2002)

All of us search for that perfect trout stream. Those
who find it treasure it the rest of their lives. Those who
don't keep on searching.
—Jimmy D. Moore, *Trout Streams I've Known*

"Did you have some fun?" I asked the terribly serious
enthusiast when he returned from upstream. He said:
"I never have fun when I fish."

—NL

Trout fishing. One must be a stickler for proper form. Use nothing but #4 blasting caps. Or a hand grenade, if handy. Or at a pool well-lined with stone, one blast from a .44 magnum will bring a few stunned brookies quietly to the surface.

—Edward Abbey

Even the thousandth trip to the same old familiar fished-out stream begins with renewed hope, with unfailing faith.

—Zane Grey

Addiction, Compulsion

Naughty little speckled trout,
Can't I coax you to come out?
Is it such great fun to play
In the water every day?
Do you pull the Naiads' hair
Hiding in the lilies there?
Do you hunt for fishes' eggs,
Or watch tadpoles grow their legs?
Do the little trouts have school
In some deep sun-glinted pool,
And in recess play at tag
Round that bed of purple flag?
I have tried so hard to catch you,
Hours and hours I've sat to watch you;
But you never will come out,
Naughty little speckled trout!

—Amy Lowell, "The Trout,"
A Dome of Many-Coloured Glass (1912)

1,001 Pearls of Fishing Wisdom

For the rich there's therapy, for the rest of us there's Fly Fishing.

—Anonymous

May his leaders rot!

—Anonymous,
a dire malediction toward an enemy or rival

May your leaders never rot!
—Anonymous, a fond hope at the close of a letter

Mankind consists of those who fish, those who are caught—and let's not forget the worms!

—Izaak Walton

Naked women could have been skydiving into a bull's eye on his head and he'd have kept on casting.
—Lorian Hemingway, "Walk on Water for Me," *A Different Angle: Fly Fishing Stories by Women* (1995)

Addiction, Compulsion

In his eye is nary a red, my boys,
But keen and well he sees;
He has a dark stripe on his side—
Micropterus salmoides.

—Fred Mather, "Big-Mouth Black Bass,"
Songs for Fishermen (1922)

The rushing stream, the angler's dream!
—William E. Elliott (as "Piscator")

And when, with trumpet to his lip,
The herald angel stands in sight,
He'll hook another worm and call,
"Wait Gabriel, just another bite!"

—W. H. Johnson, "The Inveterate Angler,"
Field & Stream (May 1909)

It puts the red blood in your veins
And sets you right with men
That's why the time can't come too soon
For fishin'—once again.

—P. S. Peck

Three-fourths of the earth is water, and one-fourth is land. It is quite clear that the good Lord intended us to spend triple the amount of time fishing as taking care of the lawn.

—Chuck Clark

The rich are comrades to the poor, out fishin';
All brothers to the common lure, out fishin'.
—Edgar A. Guest, "Out Fishin',"
The Path to Home (1919)

Addiction, Compulsion

Take my friends and my home—as an outcast I'll roam:
Take the money I have in the bank: It is just what I
Wish, but deprive me of fish
And my life would indeed be a blank!
—Lewis Carroll, "The Two Brothers" (1853)

Never leave when the fish are rising.
—Wise advice

Just one more cast . . .
—Most of us, mendaciously

When I go fishing and catch no fish, I berate myself inwardly. The pastime is seldom a relaxation for me. I must catch fish; and if I do, I must catch more.
—Ian Frazier, *The Fish's Eye: Essays about Angling and the Outdoors* (2002)

THE LIGHTER SIDE

Jim Harrison is surely right when he says that "a sense of humor is the most valuable thing an angler can own."

Wondrously comic events take place when we fish—from pratfalls to lost fish to the inevitable mendacity that collects along rivers and lakes—and a good number of the best writers have either recorded these moments or given us the words to see some aspect of the angling passion from a distinctly comical angle. I once knew a very serious fly fisher who insisted that he never had "fun" when he fly fished: it was simply too serious a matter for him. Pity. He missed much. All fishing can be lots of fun—especially when we see some of our own foibles and fetishes, our hyperbole and exaggeration. Ed Zern, who dominates this section, knew this and so do many others, including such wonderful writers as John Gierach, Richard Brautigan, Corey Ford, Robert Traver, and dozens of others.

The Lighter Side

I suspect that a sense of humor is the most valuable thing an angler can own.

—Jim Harrison

It has always been my private conviction that any man who puts his intelligence up against a fish and loses it had it coming.

—John Steinbeck, *America and Americans* (1966)

Fishermen are born honest, but they get over it.

—Ed Zern, *To Hell with Fishing* (1945)

You can always tell a fisherman, but you can't tell him much.

—Corey Ford

Want to see a fish get a hernia? Go dapping.

—Robert H. Boyle, *Dapping: The Exciting Way of Fishing Flies that Fly, Quiver and Jump* (2007)

233

1,001 Pearls of Fishing Wisdom

My nerves are strung, my teeth are set,
My brow and more of me is wet
With what is surely honest sweat.
Who christened this the "gentle art"?
—Alfred Cochrane, "Fresh Run," *Collected Verses* (1905)

Lo the angler. He is riseth in the morning and
upsetteth the whole household. Mighty are his
preparations. He goeth forth with great hope in his
heart—and when the day is far spent he returneth,
smelling of strong drink, and the truth is not in him.

　　　　　　　　　　　　　　　　　—Anonymous

Between them, the old men must have created
hundreds of trout flies, insect mutants as bizarre and
seductive as any ever to drop from a fly tier's vise.
With perhaps two exceptions, none of their titillating
offerings ever stirred a trout's interest, a fact that
didn't bother them at all.
—Harry Middleton, *The Earth Is Enough: Growing Up
in a World of Flyfishing, Trout & Old Men* (1989)

The Lighter Side

By then, I had sufficiently annoyed the pool of fish that one retaliated by striking my lure.

—Nancy Lord, "Magadan Luck,"
Uncommon Waters (1991)

Most fishing rods work better if you grasp them at the thick end. If you grasp a fisherman at the thick end, you might get a thumb bit off.

—Ed Zern, *How to Tell Fish from Fishermen* (1947)

Trout thrive best in water with a high mineral content, while this is the very sort of water that is worst for making Tennessee whiskey. This is why one never finds a trout in a fifth of Jack Daniel's. Or vice versa.

—Milford Stanley Poltroon

"I'm curious about the trout stream you have for sale. Can you tell me something about it? How are you selling it?"

"We're selling it by the foot length. You can buy as little as you want or you can buy all we've got left. . . . We're selling the waterfalls separately, of course."

—Richard Brautigan, *Trout Fishing in America* (1967)

Here's a guy standing in water up to his liver, throwing the world's most expensive clothes line at the trees.

—P. J. O'Rourke

I make it a rule never to weigh or measure a fish I've caught, but simply to estimate its dimensions as accurately as possible, and then, when telling about it, to improve those figures by roughly a fifth, or 20 percent. I do this mainly because most people believe all fishermen exaggerate by at least 20 percent, and so I allow for the discounting my audience is almost certain to apply.

—Ed Zern, "Are Fishermen Really Liars?" (1977)

The Lighter Side

Most fishermen swiftly learn that it's a pretty good rule never to show a favorite spot to any fisherman you wouldn't trust with your wife.

—Robert Traver

Crappies are a special breed of Midwestern fish, created by God for the express purpose of surviving in waters that would kill a bubonic-plague bacillus.

—Jean Shepherd, "Hairy Gertz and the Forty-Seven Crappies," *In God We Trust, All Others Pay Cash* (1966)

Have I told you my own pet theory, the one about the influence of bald spots on trout fishing?

—Robert Traver, *Trout Madness* (1960)

A man comes into a shop and asks, "Can I have a rod and reel for my son?" The owner replies, "Sorry sir, we don't do trades."

—Anonymous

1,001 Pearls of Fishing Wisdom

Never go fishing with someone else's kid unless you enjoy kids a lot more than you do fishing.
> —John Gierach, *Trout Bum* (1986)

Stevie rose all day to cake, sandwiches, fruit, hard-boiled eggs, pickles, candy like a trout to a mayfly hatch . . .
> —Sparse Grey Hackle, *Fishless Days,*
> *Angling Nights* (1971)

To bring to gaff a salmon than a bluefin tuna I would suna.
> —Ed Zern, *How to Tell Fish from Fishermen* (1947)

. . . the tinier the fisherman's brain the easier it is for him to think like a fish and catch trout right and left. The same principle explains why fishermen with big mouths catch the most large-mouth bass . . .
> —Ed Zern, *To Hell with Fishing* (1945)

The Lighter Side

I spent the entire dream fishing a single Griffith's gnat.
—Harry Middleton, *Rivers of Memory* (1993)

It is easy to tell tourists from tarpon. Tarpon have a
narrow, bony plate inside the mouth on the lower jaw.
Tourists (especially in St. Petersburg) have both upper
and lower plates.
—Ed Zern, *How to Tell Fish from Fishermen* (1947)

Do fishermen eat avocados? This is a question know
one ever thinks to ask.
—Russell Chatham, *Dark Waters* (1988)

Fish recognize a bad leader.

—Conan O'Brien

Slapping at the fly on your face is one of the methods
for unhooking the fish.

—President Herbert Hoover,
Fishing for Fun—And to Wash Your Soul (1963)

Flyfishing is like sex, everyone thinks there is more than there is, and that everyone is getting more than their share.

—Henry Kanemoto

. . . spending more time with my fly firmly attached to the branches of trees and almost none of it attached to the lips of the trout.
    —Tom Sutcliffe, MD, *Reflections on Fishing* (1990)

If you've got short, stubby fingers and wear reading glasses, any relaxation you would normally derive from fly fishing is completely eliminated when you try to tie on a fly.

—Jack Ohman, *Fear of Fly Fishing* (1988)

The Lighter Side

We believe that flies are meant to imitate life and
steelhead flies are essentially meant to imitate a
Barbie Doll's fashion accessories—especially if you
appreciate purple Easter bunnies with black feather
boas and red clown noses.

—James R. Babb

A fish story needs no apology; and no affidavit nor
string of affidavits can add anything to its credibility.
—David Starr Jordan, *Fish Stories, Alleged and
Experienced* (1909)

. . . when the fish are not rising I recite long, sonorous
pieces of poetry to them in a loud voice, bellowing
into the wind. There is nothing that bores trout so
completely—Herder, Milton, Spencer, and Victor Hugo
are the best—and they become quite distracted,
yawn, and make so, for them, the fatal mistake.
—John Inglis Hall, *Fishing a Highland Stream* (1963)

On the Firehole I caught thirty-six inches worth of trout—in six installments.
    —Arnold Gingrich, In a letter to the author (c. 1971)

My mere presence has spoiled the fishing in half a dozen states.
—Art Scheck, *Warmwater Fly Fishing Magazine* (1998)

. . . did I ever tell you about the time I saved a trout from drowning?
    —Jim Deren, quoted by Ian Frazier, *The Fish's Eye: Essays about Angling and the Outdoors* (2002)

The Lighter Side

After several [test] casts across the grass, I was approached by a uniformed park official. "There's no fishing here, sir."

"You're telling me," I said with a smile. "I haven't caught a single thing."

"Fishing is not allowed in the park," said the earnest official.

"I am not fishing. There is no water here!"

"Well if you don't stop whatever you're doing, I'll have to write you a ticket."

"A ticket for what?"

"For fishing."

    —Walter Stuart, "Fishing Rules," Metropolitan Dairy section of *The New York Times* (January 29, 2012)

I love to put funny things on my head. Sometimes it's the nut dish, sometimes the spaghetti colander, but the hats I'd seen flyfishermen wear were funnier than either, and I had to have one.

    —P. J. O'Rourke, "Stone. Water. Insect. Fish. Sunlight.", *Los Angeles Times* (April 20, 2004)

243

If you want a trout, don't fish in a herring barrel.

—Ann Landers

The chief difference between big-game fishing and weightlifting is that weightlifters never clutter up their library walls with stuffed barbells.

—Ed Zern, *How to Tell Fish from Fishermen* (1947)

Scholars have long known that fishing eventually turns men into philosophers. Unfortunately, it is almost impossible to buy decent tackle on a philosopher's salary.

—Patrick F. McManus

Under the conditions then prevailing—the thermometer recording ninety-seven degrees in the shade, the stream at its lowest point, and the temperature of the water very high—I really believe that the only chance he might have had would have been with a very "wet" mint julep.

—George M. L. La Branche,
The Dry Fly and Fast Water (1914)

The Lighter Side

There is no use in walking five miles to fish when you can depend on being just as unsuccessful near home.
—Mark Twain

As the old fisherman remarked after explaining the various ways to attach a frog to a hook, it's all the same to the frog.
—Paul Schullery, *Mountain Time* (1984)

Contrary to a common belief, it is not true that if you cut a worm-fisherman in half, each half will grow into a complete fisherman. For which we should all be grateful.
—Ed Zern, *How to Tell Fish from Fishermen* (1947)

As far as I know, I am the only living human being who has ever caught a fish in the Seine River within the city limits of Paris.
—Ed Zern, *How to Tell Fish from Fishermen* (1947)

"Then do you mean that I have to go on catching these damned two-and-a-half pounders at this corner forever and ever?"
The keeper nodded.
"Hell!" said Mr. Castwell.
"Yes," said his keeper.
—G. E. M. Skues, "Mr. Theodore Castwell," *Sidelines, Sidelights, and Reflections* (1947)

My own experience with the Cleveland Wrecking Yard began two days ago when I heard about a used trout stream they had on sale out at the yard.
—Richard Brautigan, *Trout Fishing in America* (1967)

More voters than anyone thinks would support a Worms-for-Angling ticket. There are worse political slogans.
—F. F. Van de Water, *In Defense of Worms* (1949)

The Lighter Side

. . . it takes several years of serious fishing before a man learns enough to go through a whole season with an unblemished record of physical and spiritual anguish.

—Ed Zern, *Are Fishermen People?* (1951)

With nary one fish to show for his day with rod and reel, an amateur fisherman stopped at a market on his way home and thoughtfully bought a dozen trout. He then ordered the fish man to throw them to him one at a time. "When I tell my wife," he explained to the mystified fish man, "that I catch fish—I catch them!"

—Bennett Cerf

The truth is, fish have very little sex life. If you have ever tried to make love under water, you will know why.

—Ed Zern, *How to Tell Fish from Fishermen* (1947)

. . . of all the liars among mankind, the fisherman is the most trustworthy.

—William Sherwood Fox,
Silken Lines and Silver Hooks (1954)

The pool was but a stone's throw from the house, and I arrived there in a few minutes, only to find a boy disturbing the water by dredging it with a worm. Him I lured away with a cake of chocolate . . .

—George M. L. La Branche,
The Dry Fly and Fast Water (1914)

Don't tell fish stories where the people know you; but particularly, don't tell them where they know the fish.

—Mark Twain

Creeps and idiots cannot conceal themselves for long on a fishing trip.

—John Gierach

The Lighter Side

Somebody just back of you while you are fishing is as bad as someone looking over your shoulder while you write a letter to your girl.

—Ernest Hemingway

I have made it a matter of policy to disbelieve all fishing stories on their first telling; they being to have the ring of truth, however, after I've repeated them several times.

—Paul Quinnett

You must remember that there's plenty of salt in the sea to take with the tales your fellow fishermen tell.

—John Hersey

Some people are under the impression that all that is required to make a good fisherman is the ability to tell lies easily and without blushing. But that is a mistake. Mere bald fabrication is useless. It is in the circumstantial detail, the embellishing touches of probability, the general air of scrupulous—almost of pedantic—veracity, that the experienced angler is seen.

—Jerome K. Jerome

If the old boy [Izaak Walton] occasionally stretched the truth, it strikes me that it makes him an even more appropriate father figure for a cult whose members are often given to hyperbole.

—Robert Diendorfer

The Lighter Side

That old story about the little boy with the pin-hook, who ketched all the fish, while the gentleman with the modern improvements, who stood alongside of him, kep' throwin' out his beautiful flies and never got nothin', is a pure lie.

—Frank R. Stockton

I only hope the fish will take half as much trouble for me as I've taken for them.

—Rudyard Kipling, letter to James M. Conland (August 8, 1899)

Eel fishing is a chaotic, almost slapstick business.

—Luke Jennings, *Blood Knots* (2011)

What do the little fishes do that make most truthful men untrue?

—Joseph Morris, "Fish Stories," *Songs for Fishermen* (1922)

SOME ANGLERS

From "trout bums" to "perfect anglers" to a "river god" to the new breed of women anglers, it's always a pleasure to see quite how diverse the community of anglers has grown. Even bald facts will tell you about the level of skill some anglers have attained—like the simple report that Ellis Newman could cast a fly line ninety feet with his bare hands, or the first vision a boy has of an "old salmon fisher, fully rigged, looking every bit like a god." You'll meet bumblers and experts in this section, those who want to catch many fish or big fish or only difficult fish, those who have something to prove, others who just want to be alone on the water. As in just about everything you might say about anglers and angling, the points of view these anglers embody, their presence and their goals, will vary greatly and sometimes collide.

Some Anglers

Ellis Newman could cast a fly line to ninety feet with his bare hands.

—A. J. McClane

. . . LaBranche darting upstream like a swallow, creating artificial hatches, taking plump pounders from the most unpromising places.

—Ferris Greenslet, *Under the Bridge* (1943)

Fishing on a moonless midnight in Outer Mongolia with non-English-speaking guides who had Genghis Khan Vodka for supper takes guts.

—Jessica Maxwell, "Twelve Flew into the Cuckoo's Nest," *A Different Angle: Fly Fishing Stories by Women* (1995)

. . . even the experts get skunked, and often do, even as you and I.

—Arnold Gingrich, *The Joys of Trout* (1973)

I can remember individual days and individual fish, there isn't a cow-pound or a backwater that I can't see a picture of if I shut my eyes and think.
—George Orwell, *Coming Up for Air* (1939)

At the thick end of an immense salmon rod there strode out into the sunlight the noblest figure I had ever seen. . . . The sixteen-foot rod in hand, the deer-stalker hat, bespent with flies, crowning his shaggy head, the waders, like seven-league boots, braced up to his armpits, the creel across his shoulders, a gaff across his back, he looked like he was—a god.
—Roland Pertwee, "The River God" (1928)

Ray Bergman is a good example of a mortal who became a giant by way of a failed sporting goods store.

—Andrew Herd

Some Anglers

There is no substitute for fishing sense, and if a man doesn't have it, verily, he may cast like an angel and still use his creel largely to transport sandwiches and beer.

—Robert Traver, *Trout Madness* (1960)

Today, the face of fly fishing is changing. Women are enjoying the sport in unprecedented numbers, reinterpreting its traditions and creating some of their own.

—Holly Morris, Introduction to *A Different Angle: Fly Fishing Stories by Women* (1995)

Fishing has always been for me something private and being solitary is a part of the pleasure. I tend to go on my own and talk to the trout.

—Michael Hordern, *Gone Fishing* (1995)

1,001 Pearls of Fishing Wisdom

I came to the conclusion that to become legendary all one need to do was to catch oversized fish and not die from sunstroke or lip cancer, tie a few exotic-looking flies, cast phenomenal distances against the wind and remain steadfastly laconic when a novice is on board.

—Lorian Hemingway, "Walk on Water for Me," *A Different Angle: Fly Fishing Stories by Women* (1995)

I will never tire of what fishing gives me. It puts me in touch with another of nature's species, in beautiful surroundings that are as old as time. This is where I want to be; that is how I am renewed.

—Joan Wulff

. . . women are often better fishermen than men. Rosalyn Carter and Hadley Hemingway beat out Jimmy and Ernest on streams.

—Allison Moir, "Love the Man, Love the Fly Rod," *A Different Angle: Fly Fishing Stories by Women* (1995)

Some Anglers

There is no more graceful and healthful accomplishment for a lady than fly-fishing, and there is no reason why a lady should not in every respect rival a gentleman in the gentle art.

—W. C. Prime

I think I've spent the rest of my life searching for that fish, catching many others but never the one that got away on that fine spring day.

—Mary S. Kuss, "Jesus, Pete, It's a Woman Fly Fishing," *Uncommon Waters* (1991)

. . . you must indure worse luck sometime, or you will never make a good angler.

—Izaak Walton, *The Compleat Angler* (1653)

. . . but for the practical part, it is that that makes an Angler; it is diligence, and observation, and practice that must do it.

—Izaak Walton, *The Compleat Angler* (1653)

1,001 Pearls of Fishing Wisdom

The moment of catching a fish unites all lovers
of fishing in the same, but perhaps ultimately
indescribable joy.
—Michael Hordern, *Gone Fishing* (1995)

The true angler is generally a modest man . . .
—Thaddeus Norris,
The American Angler's Book (1864)

. . . just as I had been profoundly shocked to do better
than the great master [Halford] did on the first day, I
was fated to be similarly shocked on each of his three
other days. Yet it encouraged me to rely on my own
observations and not to attach undue importance to
authority.
—G. E. M. Skues, *Itchen Memories* (1951)

I fell in love with a fly fisherman. . . . I can't believe my
competition is a fish, and not other women.
—Allison Moir

Some Anglers

Nearly crying because nothing seemed to dislodge
the fish, I was beginning to despond, when he tugged
gently, as if to say, "Are you there?" and evidently
understanding my telegraphic assent, tore off
again . . .

—Lady Agnes Macdonald

The spirit which makes the great angler is
compounded of terrifically intense concentration and a
ferocious predatory urge to conquer and capture.
—Sparse Grey Hackle, "The Perfect Angler," *Fishless
Days, Angling Nights* (1971)

Really fine fishing eyesight is a gift of the gods, the
rarest and most enviable attribute a fisherman can
possess, and I have never known a truly great angler
who did not have it.
—Sparse Grey Hackle, "The Perfect Angler," *Fishless
Days, Angling Nights* (1971)

No one under the age of thirty qualifies as a trout bum.
   —Gary LaFontaine, Foreword to *Trout Bum* by John Gierach (1986)

John Pike was a thick-set younker, with a large and bushy head, deep blue eyes that could see through water, and the proper slouch of shoulder into which great anglers ripen . . .
   —R. D. Blackmore, "Crocker's Hole" (1895)

The only thing we have ever done together is fish. Fishing is the way we have known each other, and slenderly, silently, even then.
   —Gretchen Legler, "Fishergirl" (of her father), *A Different Angle: Fly Fishing Stories by Women* (1995)

Some Anglers

The best chum I ever had in fishing was a girl, and she tramped just as hard and fished quite as patiently as any man I ever knew.

—Theodore Gordon

It is just possible that nice guys don't catch the most fish. But they find far more pleasure in those they do get.

—Roderick L. Haig-Brown

I have long felt that mentors are what make our sport special.
—John Randolph, Foreword to *Trout Hunter: The Way of an Angler* by Rene Harrop (2003)

The love of angling increases with the lapse of years, for its love grows by what it feeds on.

—Dr. James A. Henshall,
Book of the Black Bass (1881)

I doubt if rifle, shot-gun, or fowling piece ever becomes so dear and near to the sportsman as the rod to the angler, for the rod really becomes a part of himself, as it were, through which he feels every motion of the fish when hooked . . .

—Dr. James A. Henshall,
Book of the Black Bass (1881)

For every fisherman there's a ghost fish that, along with the memory of the knot that slipped, the line that snapped, or the hook-hold that gave, will haunt his dreams forever.

—Luke Jennings, *Blood Knots* (2011)

Some Anglers

My elation at taking that particular fish was quite
beyond rational justification. I experienced an illusion
of triumph which contained not only the impression
that I had finally succeeded in outfoxing a shrewd
and calculating adversary, but that the trout had been
made to know the humiliation of defeat.

—Harold F. Blaisdell,
The Philosophical Fisherman (1969)

The true fisherman approaches the first day of fishing
with all the sense of wonder and awe of a child
approaching Christmas.

—Robert Traver, *Trout Madness* (1960)

I don't WANT to catch a fish, I felt like shouting. I
can't. I am a prisoner hemmed in by walls of trees and
branches. The long rod does not *want* to work in these
conditions. I am hot and I look absurd.

—Margot Page, *Little Rivers* (1995)

265

. . . there appear to be a few fishermen around who still can't drop a line into a teacup at fifty paces.
—H. G. Tapply, *The Sportsman's Notebook* (1964)

What a tourist terms a plague of insects, the fly fisher calls a great hatch.
—Patrick F. McManus

Chalk-stream fishing, on the days when you can't connect, is one of the most exquisitely frustrating pastimes imaginable.
—Luke Jennings, *Blood Knots* (2011)

About ninety in a hundred fancy themselves anglers. About one in a hundred is an angler.
—Colonel Peter Hawker, *Instructions to Young Sportsmen* (1814)

Some Anglers

Success on the stream or in life comes from taking a balanced approach. In the business world, successful CEOs must possess more than one skill set. This balance allows them to overcome obstacles on a daily basis. The same holds true for successful anglers.

—George Daniel

From birth to death, anyone can fish. I just think it's fantastic to see old people going fishing with young people and teaching them things. I'm very, very critical.

—Rex Hunt

. . . just a toast to trout men, one and all. There are so few left, so few who believe the earth is enough.
—Harry Middleton, *The Earth Is Enough: Growing Up in a World of Flyfishing, Trout & Old Men* (1989)

267

. . . angling is an art and an art worth your learning. The question is, rather, whether you be capable of learning it.

—Izaak Walton, *The Compleat Angler* (1653)

I read Lyons, Gierach, Traver and I understand their special torment. That unique viewpoint that forces them to dwell on their failures. That viewpoint which forces us all to examine our sport each according to his background and skill level.

—Old Rupe, "Prosit!" *Fly Anglers Online*

There's too many men fishing and not enough fish.

—Annie Proulx, *The Shipping News* (1993)

I have spent too much of my life proving I can be one of the guys, never saying uncle, never admitting I'm tired or hurting or cold.

—Pam Houston, "The Company of Men," *A Different Angle: Fly Fishing Stories by Women* (1995)

Some Anglers

More men than women fish. Sometimes this works
out fine, but other times the shadow of angry
excluded wives and girlfriends falls across the sport,
and things get depressing.

—Ian Frazier, *The Fish's Eye: Essays about Angling and
the Outdoors* (2002)

There are only two occasions when Americans
respect privacy, especially in presidents. Those are
prayer and fishing.

—President Herbert Hoover, *Fishing for Fun—And to
Wash Your Soul* (1963)

[If an Angler] has attained the higher branches of the
art, he affects to despise all sport which he considers
less scientific; if a salmon fisher, he calls trout vermin;
if he is a trout fly-fisher, he professes contempt for
bait fishing.

—Thaddeus Norris,
The American Angler's Book (1864)

One hesitates to ask another fisherman to divulge the location of a hot spot. Such knowledge is, and should be, earned.
—William Tapply, "Trout Fishing in the Battenkill River," *Yankee Magazine* (September/October 2007)

I am the Blanche DuBois of fishermen. I have always depended upon the kindness of strangers.
—John Cole, *Fishing Came First* (1989)

Lo, the fisherman's wife. All she wants is the spare bedroom back. It's covered with rods and reels, flies and vests, waders, rain gear, hooks and leaders, etc. For a trip six months from now. Not a safe place to step or sleep or rest! But honey! I want to be prepared, he says. So Lo the fisherman's wife.
—Jody Moore

Some Anglers

On W. C. Steward and H. Cholmondeley-Pennell:
Well, they have both long been dead and, I suppose,
fish the Styx, one fishing up and one fishing down and
pass each other without speaking.
    —Arthur Ransome, "Rivalries," *Rod and Line* (1929)

The time is past, I thank Providence, when it was
thought unladylike for a woman to be a good shot or a
skillful angler.
                    —Cornelia Crosby, "Fly Rod's Notebook"

Everyone gets hung up in trees or streamside brush.
Everyone. Fly fishers who tell you different are either
lying or never fish in those tricky places where the
best fish lurk.
    —Tom Rosenbauer, *The Orvis Guide to Beginning Fly
                                Fishing* (2009)

. . . the things fishermen know about trout aren't facts but articles of faith.

—John Gierach, *Trout Bum* (1986)

Bass fishing, which used to be not at all that much more uptown than coon hunting, or anyway dove shooting, has in recent years become nearly as tied up in money, tips from the tops (pros hold "bass seminars" at men's clubs), official memberships, and shiny new equipment as has golf.

—Roy Blount, Jr.

Some Anglers

As our skill increases we reach the third stage, that of caring for skill for its own sake and less entirely for the results. There comes to be some satisfaction in doing things well, even when the results are not great, in continuing to throw a long line straight and lightly even when fish are rising badly . . .

—Lord Edward Grey of Fallondon, *Fly-Fishing* (1899)

I fished a little while ago with a man, not in his first youth, who had wasted the flower of his life on business and golf and gardening and motoring and marriage, and had in this way postponed his initiation far too long.

—Arthur Ransome, "On Giving Advice to Beginners," *Rod and Line* (1929)

Sad to report, the ugly American not only is alive and well, but all too frequently seems to go fly fishing.
  —George Black, *Casting a Spell: The Bamboo Fly Rod and the American Pursuit of Perfection* (2006)

All good fishermen stay young until they die, for fishing is the only dream of youth that doth not grow stale with age.

  —J. W. Muller

Some Anglers

To start with you try to catch more trout than any other fellow angler, you then progress to catching bigger trout than anyone else, and eventually you are only happy catching those very difficult educated trout that have eluded all others.

—John Goddard, *John Goddard's Trout Fishing Techniques: Practical Fly Fishing Solutions* (1996)

A LITTLE ABOUT GUIDES,
TOURNAMENTS, AND
PROFESSIONAL
MATTERS

One writer here notes the irony of doing something for a living that most people do for the sheer pleasure of it. And doing it over and over and over. Does the financial part destroy the emotional connection? Does the expert *have* to catch fish all the time? Is tournament fishing no worse or better than playing football or golf or chess for the money? Walton speaks of the "harmless art of angling," but some of what happens on the water today is governed by ferocious competition. A few anglers distrust all experts; others rightly take great pleasure in learning to cast with more authority or looking into the fish's world more perceptively. Guides can be indispensable in certain fishing occasions; tournaments are exciting to some, abominations to others; and some folk have had fine years in some aspect of a professional angling life, writing or editing or making or selling.

Guides, Tournaments, and Professional Matters

A good fishing guide will begin to size up the angler right away. Is he talkative? Can he take advice? Does he have much experience?

—Peter Kaminsky, *The Fly Fisherman's Guide to the Meaning of Life* (2008)

My first several years in the media racket were on long, tiring lesson in disenchantment. I wasn't ready for famous authors who can't string six words together without making seven mistakes, for advertisers who want "editorial support" in exchange for buying space . . . for companies willing to swap free equipment or trips for glowing write-ups . . .

—Art Scheck, *A Fishing Life is Hard Work* (2003)

"They come, they go, they feed, they stop feeding. The biggest fish can have the subtlest takes." Of such nostrums are the hours between hook-ups often filled: They are an essential part of the successful guide's tool kit.

> —Peter Kaminsky, "Trout Fresh From the Sea at the End of the Earth in Argentina," *The New York Times* (May 20, 2009)

It takes planning, effort, money, airplanes, a van ride down a rutted sandy track, and finally a flat boat to deliver you and your guide to that moment when a fish appears.

> —Bill Lambot

I distrust experts in general and fishing experts in particular.

> —W. D. Wetherell, *Vermont River* (1984)

Guides, Tournaments, and Professional Matters

Any time a professional fish writer complains about his job, the world is rightfully licensed to kick his butt until he shuts up and realizes he isn't exactly leading a life of quiet desperation out there on the Deschutes or the Tay or the Golfo Duce.
   —James R. Babb, "Home Away From Home," *Gray's Sporting Journal* (May/June 2005)

The guys and gals working here don't try to bowl anyone over with Latin. They've all had to check their ego at the employee entrance. . . . We know the answers, and we still remember when we were on the asking end of those types of questions.
                              —The Fly Shop, 2012 Catalog

The angler who is determined to catch the biggest fish or the most of them, by his own determination becomes a competitor and is self-poisoned.
                              —John Atherton, *The Fly and the Fish*

281

When a man is hired as a guide his responsibility is to see that the angler he's guiding gets the best possible service.
—Ray Bergman, "Ray Bergman Says Goodbye,"
Fishing with Ray Bergman (1970)

. . . a long immersion in the business of fishing can do things to a fisherman. Some guys burn out and turn their backs on both the business and the sport. Others become cynical hacks or shills for manufacturers. A few become drunkards.
—Art Scheck, *A Fishing Life is Hard Work* (2003)

Within three years after starting my first job at an angling magazine, I'd stopped fishing. . . . Spiders built webs between the rod tubes . . .
—Art Scheck, *A Fishing Life is Hard Work* (2003)

Catching a fish in front of clients is a big no-no,
especially if they haven't caught any yet.
—Jennifer Smith, "Paul Bunyan: My Wooly Bugger
  Chucking Machine," *Uncommon Waters* (1991)

My early and ingenuous ideas about the role of a
fishing guide turned out to be totally wrong: I had
imagined it as a life rich with independence, and
with a rustic sort of dignity, wherein a fellow would
stand closer to these particular animals he admired
inordinately. I hadn't foreseen that it would demand
the humility of a chauffeur and the complaisance of a
pimp.
—David Quammen, "Stone. Water. Insect. Fish.
  Sunlight.", *Los Angeles Times* (April 20, 2004)

So listen, kid: Never keep more fish than you can eat at one meal, never eat more than you want, never want more than you need, never need more than is reasonable, never be too reasonable about what you love, never love anything so much you love it to death, never destroy what can't be replaced, never think everything can be replaced.

—Bob Shacochis, "How to Eat a Fish," *Outside Magazine* (July 1, 2000)

I am not so much objecting to the tournaments themselves . . . as to the attitudes they represent, certainly about fishing but indirectly about our notions of leisure and recreation.

—Ted Leeson, *Inventing Montana: Dispatches from the Madison Valley* (2009)

It's subscribing to the proposition that what's good for the trout and salmon is good for the fisherman and that managing trout and salmon for themselves rather than the fisherman is fundamental to our trout and salmon problems.

—Trout Unlimited Philosophy

The fish you release is your gift to another angler and, remember, it may have been someone's similar gift to you.

—Lee Wulff, *Lee Wulff's Handbook of Freshwater Fishing* (1939)

All the romance of trout fishing exists in the mind of the angler and is in no way shared by the fish.

—Harold F. Blaisdell,
The Philosophical Fisherman (1969)

285

[C]amaraderie and sportsmanship seem to have gotten lost along the way and replaced with big money tournament payouts.

—Ronald Lindner, "Twenty Questions with Fishing Legends Ronald and Al Lindner," interviewed by Juls Davis, *Walleye Central* (2011)

Greedy little minds are ever busy turning landscapes into slag heaps, housing tracts, canals, freeways and shopping malls, a perversion they zealously pursue under the ragged banner of progress.

—Sheridan Anderson, *The Curtis Creek Manifesto* (1978)

The San Juan: a river in danger of being loved to death for all the right reasons.

—Steven J. Meyers, *San Juan River Chronicle* (1994)

The Campbell I know almost as a man should know a river.

—Roderick L. Haig-Brown,
A River Never Sleeps (1946)

I am a Brother of the Angle, and therefore an enemy to the otter . . .

—Izaak Walton, *The Compleat Angler* (1653)

In 1918 I realized that the growing use of the automobile, with its easy transportation, would soon spoil all public trout fishing . . .

—Edward R. Hewitt, *A Trout and Salmon Fisherman for Seventy-Five Years* (1948)

There is a cost to a fish in being caught, even if it is promptly released.
—Paul Guernsey, *Beyond Catch & Release* (2011)

Fly fishing offers the comfort of ritual, harbors a strict code of ethics, and inspires a pantheistic philosophy in its devotees.
—Holly Morris, *A Different Angle: Fly Fishing Stories by Women* (1995)

Why burden a beginning angler with physically demanding or fussy techniques under tough conditions when all he wants to do is catch any sort of fish?
—Jerry Gibbs, "Backup Plans Be Prepared to Catch Whatever Will Bite," *Outdoor Life*

The line between catching fish and not catching them is often very thin.
> —Ted Trueblood, *Field & Stream* (1952)

. . . the most honest, ingenious, harmless art of Angling.
> —Izaak Walton, *The Compleat Angler* (1653)

Anything was fish that came to my net.
> —Gilbert Keith Chesterton, "A Fish Story," *The Collected Short Works of G. K. Chesterton* (1986)

It is only the inexperienced and thoughtless who find pleasure in killing fish for the mere sake of killing them. No sportsman does this.
> —W. C. Prime

. . . so here's to you a hearty draught, and to all that love us, and the honest art of Angling.

—Izaak Walton, *The Compleat Angler* (1653)

One of the reasons I love to fly fish is the relaxing rhythm of the sport—the total removal in place, and purpose, from the stress and competition of work.

—Judy Muller, "Only One Fly," *A Different Angle: Fly Fishing Stories by Women* (1995)

Fly-fishing, or any other sport fishing, is an end in itself and not a game or competition among fishermen . . .

—Ed Zern, "The Ethics, Perhaps, of Fly Fishing," *Fifty Years of Ed Zern* (2003)

There is also a sort of gambler's comradeship aboard the boats. . . . John's fish was the winner; he was awarded a prize of $1,284, making his cod worth almost $38 a pound.

—Albert C. Jensen

Fly-fishing is solitary, contemplative, misanthropic, scientific in some hands, poetic in others, and laced with conflicting aesthetic considerations. It is not even clear if catching fish is actually the point.
—John Gierach, *Dances with Trout* (1994)

I'm not sure that you do see them. You see something. The angle of a fin, a line of color, something that doesn't quite fit the background, and your brain manufactures the rest.
—Mallory Burton, "Green River Virgins," *Green River Virgins: And Other Passionate Anglers* (2000)

I've gone fishing thousands of times in my life, and I have never once felt unlucky or poorly paid for those hours on the water.
—William Tapply, *A Fly-Fishing Life* (1997)

Yes, we like to hook the fish, to fight it to submission, to bring it to our hand, to remove the fly from its mouth, to cradle it in the water while it regains its strength, and to release it and watch it swim away. If we fail to hook the fish that takes our fly, or if it breaks off or comes unbuttoned after we hook it, we are disappointed. But really, isn't all of that anticlimactic? Shouldn't the coup be counted when the fish tries to eat the fly?

—William Tapply, "Counting Coup," *American Angler* (December 8, 2010)

Game fish are too valuable to be caught only once.
—Lee Wulff, *Lee Wulff's Handbook of Freshwater Fishing* (1939)

I know of no committed fly fisher who is not a conservationist by temperament.
—John Randolph, Foreword to *Trout Hunter: The Way of an Angler* by Rene Harrop (2003)

Guides, Tournaments, and Professional Matters

The real competition in fly fishing today is for space and opportunity on public waters.

—Rene Harrop, *Trout Hunter: The Way of an Angler* (2003)

I object to fishing tournaments less for what they do to the fish than what they do to the fishermen.

—Ted Williams

Catch-and-release fishing is an ecological necessity, not my preference. The practice smacks of bad faith, an inauthentic act.

—Christopher Camuto, "Caught by the Way," *In Praise of Wild Trout* (1998)

We have reached the time in the life of the planet, and humanity's demands upon it, when every fisherman will have to be a riverkeeper, a steward of marine shallows, a watchman on the high seas.

—Thomas McGuane, *The Longest Silence* (1999)

The greatest thrill for the most experienced fisherman is the rise or strike.

—Lee Wulff

When you cut out all the cant and humbug from the game, fly-fishing is a superbly simple thing. I should know. I do it for a living.
—Oliver Kite, *Nymph Fishing in Practice* (1963)

If this were some other sport, I'd have millions in the bank instead of pennies.
—Lefty Kreh, Interview with Dave Jamieson,
Washington Post (September 19, 2010)

Guides accept payment to help clients circumvent their own ignorance. But ignorance is one of the most crucial pieces of equipment any fly fisher will ever own.
  —David James Duncan, "A Manifesto For Ignorance,"
    Outside Magazine (July 1, 2000)

The tournament scene, with all the gold chains, big mouths, and bleached blondes, wasn't my kind of scene . . . gambling and fishing don't mix.
          —Robert Cunningham, *Chasing Records:*
            An Angler's Quest (2012)

Only when the last tree has been felled, the last river poisoned, and the last fish caught, man will know that he cannot eat money.

          —Cree Indian saying

SOME MAXIMS,
THEORIES, AND
PHILOSOPHICAL
COMMENTS

There are of course thousands of maxims and bon mots and theories about fishing but perhaps the wisest is Lord Grey's insistence that the two words *least* appropriate to any philosophic statement about fishing are "always" and "never." A few I especially like in this long omnibus section are Thomas Bastard's delicious poem about the decrease of fish while the number of "fishers multiply"; the painter John Marin's recognition in a letter to a friend that he wouldn't think of "disassociating Fishing from Art—one and the same thing with me"; or perhaps John Buchan's marvelous description of fishing as "a perpetual series of occasions for hope." But there are so many others, reminding us that even the best anglers can't catch fish if the fish aren't where they're fishing, and perhaps that we might enjoy our fishing more if we didn't have to rely upon the "cooperation of the fish."

Some Maxims, Theories, and Philosophical Comments

The gods do not subtract from the allotted span of
men's lives the hours spent in fishing.
                                    —Assyrian Tablet (2000 B.C.)

There is only one theory about angling in which I have
perfect confidence, and this is that the two words
least appropriate to any statement about it are the
words "always" and "never."
   —Lord Edward Grey of Fallondon, *Fly-Fishing* (1899)

[Angling] is tightly woven in a fabric of moral, social,
and philosophical threads which are not easily rent by
the violent climate of our times.
                        —A. J. McClane, "Song of the Angler" (1967)

. . . reality is as close as the nearest river.
                                               —A. J. McClane

1,001 Pearls of Fishing Wisdom

Don't bargain for fish which are still in the water.
—Indian Proverb

Swedish researchers . . . have shown that in 59
percent of matings, the female trout fakes her orgasm.
—Brian Clarke

Fishing, if I a fisher may protest,
Of pleasures is the sweet'st, of sports the best,
Of exercises the most excellent
Of recreations the most innocent.
But now the sport is marde, and wott ye why
Fishes decrease, and fishers multiply.
—Thomas Bastard

Wouldn't think of disassociating Fishing from Art—one
and the same thing with me.
—John Marin

Some Maxims, Theories, and Philosophical Comments

As with a faint star in the night's sky, one can better understand fishing's allure by looking around it, off to the side, not right at it.

—Holly Morris

I know no sort of men less subject to melancholy than anglers.

—Colonel Robert Venables,
The Experienced Angler (1662)

The solution to any problem—work, love, money, whatever—is to go fishing, and the worse the problem, the longer the trip should be.

—John Gierach

If fishing is like religion, then fly fishing is high church.

—Tom Brokaw

. . . not everything about fishing is noble and reasonable and sane. . . . Fishing is not an escape from life, but often a deeper immersion into it, all of it, the good and the awful, the joyous and the miserable, the comic, the embarrassing, the tragic, and the sorrowful.

—Harry Middleton, *Rivers of Memory* (1993)

The craft of angling is the catching of fish, but the art of angling is its receptiveness to these connections, the art of letting one thing lead to another until, if only locally and momentarily, you realize some small completeness.

—Ted Leeson, *The Habit of Rivers* (1994)

I chose my cast, a brown march and a dun,
And ran down to the river, chasing hope.

—Wilfred S. Blunt, *A New Pilgrimage* (1889)

Some Maxims, Theories, and Philosophical Comments

. . . in angling, "always" and "never" should be given a wide berth.

—Brian Clarke

My father was very sure about certain matters pertaining to the universe. To him, all good things— trout as well as eternal salvation—come by grace and grace comes by art and art does not come easy.
—Norman Maclean, *A River Runs through It* (1976)

Only those who come to fishing later in life are born fishermen.

—Dave Hughes

1,001 Pearls of Fishing Wisdom

Modern angling is uncomfortable with the idea [at heart a form of play] and prefers to regard itself more along the lines of modern medicine, as an acutely specialized body of knowledge dispensed by a priesthood of experts.

—Ted Leeson, *Inventing Montana: Dispatches from the Madison Valley* (2009)

The years will bring their Anodyne,
But I shall never quite forget
The fish that I had counted mine
And lost before they reached the net.

—Colin Ellis, "The Devout Angler," quoted in *The Trout Fisherman's Bedside Book* by Arthur R. Macdougall, Jr. (1963)

Soon after I embraced the sport of angling I became convinced that I should never be able to enjoy it if I had to rely on the cooperation of the fish.

—Sparse Grey Hackle

Some Maxims, Theories, and Philosophical Comments

Many of the places I fish were shown to me by friends. To give them away would be a poor way to repay kindness.

—Dave Hughes

Men and fish are alike. They both get into trouble when they open their mouths.

—Jimmy D. Moore

I now believe that fishing is far more important than the fish.

—Arnold Gingrich

La Pêche est ma folie.
  —Duc de Choiseul (1761), quoted by John Waller Hills

. . . learn to pee before you put your waders on.

—Dave Hughes

A fly fishing season does not pass in which I do not find myself misguided by following one of my favourite precepts.

—Huish Edye, *The Angler and the Trout* (1945)

There is only one thing wrong with a fishing day—its staggering brevity.

—Zane Grey, quoted in "The Men Who Lived Two Lives in One" by Robert H. Boyle, *Sports Illustrated* (April 29, 1968)

Many fishermen pray in times of stress and I know that I feel nearer to God and more religious when fighting fish than at any other time.

—S. Kip Farrington, "Peru"

. . . the trout and salmon fisherman contrives to make a virtue, a fetish even, of this habitual scarcity, if not entire famine, of catchable fish.

—Louis D. Rubin, Jr., *The Even-Tempered Angler* (1983)

Some Maxims, Theories, and Philosophical Comments

I bait my hook and cast my line
And feel the best of life is mine.
  —James Whitcomb Riley, "At Broad Ripple" (1905)

It was late in April, with the river running fine and as clear as a young parson's conscience.
  —Tom Sutcliffe, MD, *Reflections on Fishing* (1990)

The fish I remembered best of all are the ones I didn't catch.
  —George Orwell, *Coming Up for Air* (1939)

On the theory of B. Jarrett Mills, who finds bait fishing more ethical than lure fishing:
The fish, Mills declares, has been made to risk its very existence without any hope of reward.
  —Louis D. Rubin, Jr.,
  The Even-Tempered Angler (1983)

1,001 Pearls of Fishing Wisdom

The strike is always a surprise.

—Bill Lambot

. . . the art of angling, the cruelest, the coldest, the stupidest of pretended sports.

—Lord Byron, Note to *Don Juan* (1818)

I wind about, and in and out,
With here a blossom sailing,
And here and there a lusty trout,
And here and there a grayling.

—Alfred Tennyson, "The Brook," *Enoch Arden and
Other Poems* (1862)

Fer if the lord made fishin', why—a feller orter fish.

—Frank L. Stanton, "A Fisherman in Town," *Songs for
Fishermen* (1922)

308

Some Maxims, Theories, and Philosophical Comments

. . . fishing, in large part, is an ongoing lesson in learning how to let go.
>—Ron P. Swegman, "The Old Line" (2010)

I love fishing. You put that line in the water and you don't know what's on the other end. Your imagination is under there.

>—Robert Altman

The truth always sounds better and in the case of a fish story, truth is often stranger than fish fiction.
>—Henry Abbott, *Fish Stories* (1919)

I dislike killing trout but I believe that, in order to fish responsibly, to fish conscionably, the fisherman should at least occasionally kill.
>—David Quammen, "Stone. Water. Insect. Fish. Sunlight.", *Los Angeles Times* (April 20, 2004)

. . . in fishing, languor is fatal.

—Ferris Greenslet

The mood of the actual fishing is the same everywhere. It is always a restrained and muted fierceness.

—Ferris Greenslet

Were it possible to take a limit of trout every time we fished our favorite stream, how long would it take before the sport began to pall?

—Art Flick, *Art Flick's Streamside Guide to Naturals and their Limitations* (1947)

Fishing rule #1: The least experienced fisherman always catches the biggest fish.
Fishing rule #2: The worse your line is tangled, the better is the fishing around you.

—Anonymous

Some Maxims, Theories, and Philosophical Comments

What is most emphatic in angling is made so by the
long silences—the unproductive periods.
      —Thomas McGuane, *The Longest Silence* (1999)

Fishing consists of a series of misadventures
interspersed by occasional moments of glory.
      —Howard Marshall, *Reflections on a River* (1967)

. . . there is nothing clinical about fishing . . . there
is nothing about it that can be viewed in a clinical
vacuum. Everything—as in everything else—relates to
everything else; and the deeper down one goes, the
nearer the quick of life one draws.
      —Brian Clarke, *The Pursuit of the*
Stillwater Trout (1975)

Mother Nature is not fooled by technological fixes.
      —Robert Behnke, "Wild Trout and Native Trout—Is
There a Difference?" *In Praise of Wild Trout* (1998)

$E = \frac{1}{2}mv^2$

Fortunately this is translatable. It means: If a trout doubles the speed with which he darts up at a fly, he is putting out four times the amount of energy.
　　　　—J. W. Dunne, *Sunshine and the Dry Fly* (1924)

You can't play a Bach solo partita on the fly rod . . . but a split bamboo fly rod, used well, is also a small embodiment of human grace.
　　—George Black, *Casting a Spell: The Bamboo Fly Rod and the American Pursuit of Perfection* (2006)

No angler merely watches nature in a passive way. He enters into its very existence.
　　—John Bailey, *Reflections on the Water's Edge* (1987)

Some Maxims, Theories, and Philosophical Comments

Of companions: . . . the ideal is someone who is not only keep and competent, but curious, reflective, well read in the literature of the subject, who considers fishing not a competitive sport but a branch of philosophy, who takes as much pleasure in your fish as you do in his.

—Ferris Greenslet

Which of these is the wisest and happiest—he who labors without ceasing and only obtains, with great trouble, enough to live on, or he who rests in comfort and finds all that he needs in the pleasure of hunting and fishing?

—Micmac Chief

In this sport of catching fish I like to do the entire job myself.

—Lee Wulff, *Fishing with Lee Wulff* (1972)

313

Fishing is the part of life that's filled with more or less regular successes, and failures that don't really matter because there's always a next time. You come to see that a life frittered away with sport and travel makes perfect sense, but no one trip ever tells the whole story.

—John Gierach, *Another Lousy Day in Paradise* (1996)

A mark of all the best fishermen I have know has been the power of concentration, and this, perhaps, is the most important single quality a fisherman can have.

—Roderick L. Haig-Brown,
A River Never Sleeps (1946)

. . . bottom fishing . . . is a distinctive way of looking at the world.

—Louis D. Rubin, Jr.,
The Even-Tempered Angler (1983)

Some Maxims, Theories, and Philosophical Comments

It was not for nothing that a canon law of the ancient church prescribed fishing for the clergy as being "favorable to the health of the body, and especially of their souls."

—Romilly Fedden, *Golden Days* (1919)

Fishing is like that. It keeps you off balance, surprises you. It takes humility to learn, to accept that you may need a lesson or two even in your advanced stage of enlightenment.

—Kevin Nelson,
The Angler's Book of Daily Inspiration (1997)

Success begets confidence and confidence begets success—and that fine upward spiral is the best restorative of streamside sanity.

—Howard T. Walden II, *Upstream and Down* (1938)

New jobs are like hooked fish: they feel big at first but tend to be smaller once you get to know them.

—Chinese Proveb

Anglers have a way of romanticizing their battles with fish.

—Ernest Hemingway

All of us, even the experts, would be bored blind in no time at all if all our little tricks worked every time we essayed them.

—Arnold Gingrich, *The Joys of Trout* (1973)

What brings us back [to fishing] is its glorious uncertainty.

—Arnold Gingrich, *The Joys of Trout* (1973)

316

Some Maxims, Theories, and Philosophical Comments

. . . I had thought it was all foolishness, this man's business of fighting a fish. But it is not. . . . And you *do* begin to love the fish because all the pain you are going through just to keep him on the line is equal to the pain he feels in his attempts to love the thing that has gripped him.

—Lorian Hemingway, "The Young Woman and the Sea," *Uncommon Waters* (1991)

Standing in light, I cast into darkness where a trout might rest—cool, still, hidden—waiting for a morsel to tempt him into movement.

—Le Anne Schreiber, "The Long Light," *Uncommon Waters* (1991)

Do not despair. There was—alas! That I must say there was—an illustrious philosopher, who was nearly the age of fifty before he made angling a pursuit, yet he became a distinguished fly-fisher.

—Sir Humphrey Davy

317

[I]t's worth pausing to take a snapshot of our own age of angling in all its ambivalence, before the image is enhanced, cropped, synthetically patinated, and otherwise Photoshopped into memory.

—Ted Leeson, "The Best of Times, the Worst of Times," *Gray's Sporting Journal* (April 2008)

If the fish had not opened its mouth, it would not have been caught!

—Proverb

The whole notion of fly-fishing would not be so romantic if the trout did not win, too.

—Mark Rauschenberger, "Humbling Reminder," *This Is Fly* (April/May 2012)

Some Maxims, Theories, and Philosophical Comments

[F]or the maxim holds good in the matter of fishing as in everything else: the first step to be wise is to know that we are ignorant.

—Edward Hamilton, MD, *Recollections of fly fishing for salmon, trout, and grayling* (1891)

There's a fine line between fishing and standing on the shore like an idiot.

—Steven Wright

Rivers and the inhabitants of the watery elements are made for wise men to contemplate and for fools to pass by without consideration.

—Izaak Walton

Some go to church and think about fishing, others go fishing and think about God.

—Tony Blake

One brisk morning spent fishing on a misty lake can bring home to a child the beauty, drama and fragility of our natural heritage in a way a thousand classroom presentations never could.

—President George H. W. Bush, message on the observance of National Fishing Week (1989)

To talk much and arrive nowhere is the same as climbing a tree to catch a fish.

—Chinese Proverb

Bragging may not bring happiness, but no man having caught a large fish goes home through an alley.

—Author unknown

Some Maxims, Theories, and Philosophical Comments

. . . fishermen constitute a separate class or sub-race among the inhabitants of the earth.
> —President Grover Cleveland

Fishing is not like billiards, in which it is possible to attain a disgusting perfection.
> —Arthur Ransome, "On Giving Advice to Beginners," *Rod and Line* (1929)

But ah, to fish with a worm, and then not catch your fish! To fail with a fly is no disgrace: Your art may have been impeccable, your patience faultless to the end. But the philosophy of worm-fishing is that of results, of having something tangible in your basket when the day's work is done.
> —Bliss Perry, *Fishing with a Worm* (1904)

This salt-water fly fishing, it is for men with hard stomachs, like sex after lunch.
—Charles Ritz, To Author, At Lunch (c. 1972)

You must cultivate an eye for water and an eye for trout. The gift is not easily attained: In all cases it requires practice, and some never acquire it.
—John Waller Hills, *A Summer on the Test* (1930)

Some Maxims, Theories, and Philosophical Comments

. . . this winter I'm determined for once to fish sensibly, and by that I mean in comfort, to try not only to match the hatch but also to match the weather.
—Tom Sutcliffe, MD, *Reflections on Fishing* (1990)

. . . impatient sportsmen blame their bad luck.
—Sergei Aksakov, *Notes on Fishing* (1847), translated by Thomas P. Hodge (1997)

THE FISHING IN PRINT,
THE WISDOM OF YEARS

I once spoke to a group of anglers about my love of fishing books, and when I had ended a sturdy fellow stood up and said, "Once read a book about fishing. Never read another." Then he sat down. Somewhere in my talk I had mentioned Sparse Grey Hackle's observation that some of "the best fishing is done not in water but in print," and yet I know perfectly well that scores of anglers don't read books and don't miss doing so. Some of my best friends—to borrow that old phrase—fish with great passion and skill but have absolutely no interest in fishing books. Still, reading a lot of books about angling and writing a few myself has increased my pleasure on the water, and I think it can do the same for many others who love to fish. Perhaps some of the words here will intrigue you enough to try a few of those mentioned in the Bibliography.

The Fishing in Print, the Wisdom of Years

The best fishing is done not in the water but in print.
—Sparse Grey Hackle, *Great Fishing Tackle Catalogs of
the Golden Age* (1971)

The number and excellence of books devoted to the
exposition of Angling are so great that no other sport
can compare with it in these respects.
—James Robb, *Notable Angling Literature* (1947)

I bristle when a kiss-and-tell writer mentions a spot
that I have known and loved for years.

—Dave Hughes

I started writing simply because I loved fishing and
wanted to share what I learned from my endless
experiments with fishing tackle and tactics.
—Ray Bergman, "Ray Bergman Says Goodbye,"
Fishing with Ray Bergman (1970)

Trout by Ray Bergman captured my imagination, introducing me to the vast number of places to fish and techniques to master and stimulating a voracious hunger for all the literature of fly fishing.
> —Jack Hemingway, *A Life Worth Living: The Adventures of a Passionate Sportsman* (2002)

Fishing books should ooze from a riverbank, not rocket out of publisher's offices in big cities.
> —Neil Patterson, *Chalkstream Chronicles* (1995)

The literature of angling falls into two genres: the instructional and the devotional. The former is written by fishermen who write, the latter by writers who fish.
> —William Humphrey, *My Moby Dick* (1978)

The Fishing in Print, the Wisdom of Years

Fishing books, lit by emotion recollected in tranquility,
are like poetry. . . . We do not think of them as books
but as men. They are our companions and not only
riverside. Summer and winter they are with us and
what a pleasant company they are.

    —Arthur Ransome, *The Fisherman's Library* (1959)

Certainly I for one have always been attracted to the
old writers, since I first knew them, and the more I
have fished, the better I seem to understand them.

    —John Waller Hills, *A Summer on the Test* (1930)

I cannot imagine anybody writing a whole book about
maggots, whereas many a man has spent his life
thinking and writing about fisherman's flies.

    —Arthur Ransome, *The Fisherman's Library* (1959)

A run of fishless days will have me believing that I
am hexed, that almost every move I make has some
unlucky significance.

    —Howard T. Walden II, *Upstream and Down* (1938)

1,001 Pearls of Fishing Wisdom

Over the years, whenever I've felt that little winkle in the hairs on the back of my neck, as I encountered an original thought or observation in a fishing book, I've turned the corner of the page down.

—Arnold Gingrich, *The Fishing in Print: A Guided Tour through Five Centuries of Angling Literature* (1974)

I know there are some things I've read that come to mind more often while I'm fishing than anything I can remember that anybody said beside me on stream or pond.

—Arnold Gingrich, *The Fishing in Print* (1974)

For while trout fisherman's efforts are ostensibly aimed at taking trout, his preoccupation is concerned with preserving the illusion that his elaborate methodology is at all times justified.

—Harold F. Blaisdell, *The Philosophical Fisherman* (1969)

. . . perhaps the greatest satisfaction on the first day of the season is the knowledge in the evening that the whole of the rest of the season is to come.
—Arthur Ransome, "The First Day at the River," *Rod and Line* (1929)

. . . next to fishing itself, there is nothing better than a good fishing book.
—Steve Raymond, *The Year of the Trout* (1995)

I imagine no art has ever been learned from books. Fly fishing is no exception.
—G. E. M. Skues

I have learned through experience, not untinged with bitterness, that the writer on angling matters who dares the *absolute* is inviting both censure and a mountain of mail.

—Raymond R. Camp, Introduction to *Art Flick's New Streamside Guide to Naturals and their Limitations* (2007)

. . . next to the pleasure of reading a favourite fishing book comes that of persuading a friend to read it too.

—Arthur Ransome, *The Fisherman's Library* (1959)

Every angler ought to keep a record or diary of his angling bouts. . . . Reading therefrom years after at the fireside he will detect a faint perfume of old forests in the winter air.

—Frank S. Pickney, "Winter Angling," *Fishing with the fly, Sketches by lovers of the art* by Charles F. Orvis (1883)

332

The Fishing in Print, the Wisdom of Years

The ancients wrote of the three ages of man; I propose to write of the three ages of the fisherman. When he wants to catch all the fish he can. When he strives to catch the largest fish. When he studies to catch the most difficult fish he can find, requiring the greatest skill and most refined tackle, caring more for the sport than the fish.

—Edward R. Hewitt, *A Trout and Salmon Fisherman for Seventy-Five Years* (1948)

In the autumn, fishing is coming to an end, and each day you are parting with it—for a long time, for a whole six months.

—Sergei Aksakov, "Memoir," translated by Arthur Ransome

MORE THAN TO FISH

When we have fished for some years, most of us begin to think not only of the ways in which we can catch more and bigger and even more difficult fish, but also about matters that only begin with the fishing itself. We may think of our attachment to the natural world, made more immediate through fishing; we may think about our feelings when we fish, matters of friendship and mystery and adventure, and even spiritual matters; we may value that fishing is a respite from the affairs of the rest of our lives.

Izaak Walton may have the last word on this—but you will find that a great number of very wise contemporary writers weigh in on all that is truly more than only to fish.

I especially like the way conservation is closely allied to all that is more than to fish. Paul Guernsey's new book *Beyond Catch & Release* looks toward deeper issues than merely returning some or all of the fish we catch—though "merely" is a true beginning to most conservation issues connected to fishing. Lee Wulff's concept that a fish is too valuable to be caught once is a brilliant start, but it must be advanced by true knowledge and action on matters connected to the land that surrounds all water, to the water itself, and to the nature of our appreciation of what exists and what must be protected.

. . . tis not all of fishing to fish.
 —Izaak Walton, *The Compleat Angler* (1653)

The music of angling is more compelling to me than anything contrived in the greatest symphony hall.
 —A. J. McClane, "Song of the Angler" (1967)

. . . it isn't the fishing itself that is so important to me any longer but the idea of going fishing.
 —Brian Clarke

Catching and releasing wild trout is not just a sport or game, it is letting the cycle continue.
 —Ailm Travler

Fish come and go, but it is the memory of afternoons on the stream that endure.
 —E. Donnall Thomas

More than to Fish

. . . if I take my problems fishing and leave them
behind out there, they are not waiting for me when I
get back home.

—Dave Hughes

Fly fishing . . . a cheerer of the spirits, a tranquilliser of
the mind, a calmer of unquiet thoughts, a diverter of
sadness.

—Henry Wooton

Only those become weary of angling who bring
nothing to it but the idea of catching fish.

—Rafael Sabatini

Fishing is a quest for knowledge and wonder as much
as a pursuit of fish; it is as much an acquaintance
with beavers, dippers, and other fishermen as it is the
challenge of catching trout.

—Paul Schullery, *Mountain Time* (1984)

1,001 Pearls of Fishing Wisdom

All the charm of the angler's life would be lost but for these hours of thought and memory. . . . All the long evenings in camp, or cottage, or inn, he tells stories of his own life, hears stories of his friends' lives, and if alone calls up the magic of memory.

—W. C. Prime

Don't count the hours by the number of trout caught. . . . Catch that day and hold onto it.

—Jack Denton Scott

The old man used to say that the best part of hunting and fishing was the thinking about going and the talking about it after you got back.

—Robert Ruark, *The Old Man and the Boy* (1957)

When I'm fishing well, my concentration is so intensely focused on the surface of the stream that I enter a kind of trance, from which I emerge startled by some sudden sound or change in light.

—Le Anne Schreiber

More than to Fish

No political aspirant can qualify for election unless he demonstrates he is a fisherman.

>—President Herbert Hoover

. . . what the deep-dyed surf-caster always longs for— just the sea and himself.

>—Negley Farson

Had all pens that go trout fishing devoted themselves to jotting down notes about why the big fish did not gobble the grasshopper, we should have lost many a page of sunshine, fresh air, and good fellowship, and reaped a crop of fireside Disko troops who thought like the fish.

>—William McFarland

. . .the good of having wisely invested so much time in wild country . . .

>—Harry Middleton, *Rivers of Memory* (1993)

You'd think it damned silly, no doubt, but I've actually half a wish to go fishing even now, when I'm fat and forty-five, and got two kids in a house in the suburbs.
　　　　　　　　　—George Orwell, *Coming Up for Air* (1939)

For the supreme test of a fisherman is not how many fish he has caught, not even how he has caught them, but what he has caught when he has caught no fish.
　　　　　　　　　　　　　　　　　—John H. Bradley

There stood Ktaadn with distinct and cloudless outline in the moonlight; and the rippling of the rapids was the only sound to break the stillness. Standing on the shore, I once more cast my line into the stream, and I found the dream to be real and the fable true.
　　　　　　　　　—Henry David Thoreau, "Ktaadn,"
　　　　　　　　　　The Maine Woods (1864)

More than to Fish

Mergansers travel in damnable family flocks, and are rapacious . . . I have to remind myself that they are an elemental part of nature, that they have helped hone the trout into something I love, that they're eating my fish, but I am the one who belongs there least.

—Dave Hughes, *Reading the Water: A Fly Fisher's Handbook for Finding Trout in All Types of Water* (1988)

The thrill of a fish at the end of the line, that thing that sparks from the dark water to spinal cord, is a vestige of an archetypal joy that has to do with sustenance, material and spiritual.

—Christopher Camuto,
A Fly Fisherman's Blue Ridge (2001)

When I grew tired of fishing, I'd lie face down on the ties, watching for fish in the shadow-striped water below.

—Mallory Burton, "Mentors,"
Uncommon Waters (1991)

Hunting and fishing put us to the sternest kinds of moral and ethical tests.
>   —W. Hardback McLoughlin, "Decisions," *Field & Stream* (August 1994)

[Y]ou must not use this aforesaid artful sport for covetousness to increasing or saving of your money only, but principally for your solace and to promote the health of your body and specially of your soul.
>   —Dame Juliana Berners, *The Treatyse of Fishing with an Angle* (1496)

The outdoor life pleased these old men because they believed any properly obsessed fly fisherman carried rivers and trout inside him.
>   —Harry Middleton, *The Earth Is Enough: Growing Up in a World of Flyfishing, Trout & Old Men* (1989)

344

More than to Fish

. . . when the lawyer is swallowed up with business
and the statesman is preventing or contriving plots,
then we sit on cowslip-banks, hear the birds sing,
and possess ourselves in as much quietness as these
silent silver streams . . .

> —Izaak Walton, *The Compleat Angler* (1653)

The real competition in fly fishing today is for space
and opportunity on public waters.
> —Rene Harrop, *Trout Hunter: The Way of an Angler* (2003)

You can't say enough about fishing. Though the sport
of kings, it's just what the deadbeat ordered.

> —Thomas McGuane, in *Silent Seasons* (1978)

Fishing is to be enjoyed, but it will not be enjoyed any
the more by hurrying past what Nature has to give us
on the way.

> —Colonel Robert Venables,
> *The Experienced Angler* (1662)

When the heated and soiled and jaded refugee from the city first sees [the stream], he feels as if he would like to turn it into his bosom and let it flow through him a few hours, it suggests such healing freshness and newness.

—John Burroughs, *Locusts and Wild Honey* (1879)

As the angler looks back, he thinks less of individual captures and days than of scenes in which he fished.

—Lord Edward Grey of Fallondon

We may say of angling as Dr. Boteler said of strawberries:
"Doubtless God could have made a better berry, but doubtless God never did, and so, if I might be judge, God never did make a more calm, quiet, innocent recreation than angling."

—Izaak Walton, *The Compleat Angler* (1653)

More than to Fish

'Tis not a proud desire of mine;
I ask for nothing superfine;
No heavy weight, no salmon great,
To break the record or my line:
Only an idle little stream
Whose amber waters softly gleam,
Where I may wade, through woodland shade,
And cast the fly, and loaf and dream.
Only a trout or two, to dart
From foaming pools, and try my art:
No more I'm wishing, old-fashioned fishing,
And just a day on nature's heart.
  —Henry Van Dyke, "An Angler's Wish in Town" (1894)

Stalking along from long to long, or plunging their long
legs in the oozy swamp, [two large herons] paid no
attention to my presence, but occupied themselves
with their own fishing arrangements, as if their
wilderness were their own.
                    —W. C. Prime, *I Go A-Fishing* (1873)

1,001 Pearls of Fishing Wisdom

Back in the 1960s, anglers didn't care about stream flows and river habitat, because if the fishing was poor, you just tossed in more fish.

> —Dick Vincent, Interview by *Montana Outdoors* (May/June 2004)

Honestly, there are times when I could care less if I catch anything at all.

> —Allen Jones, *Big Sky Journal*

Calling fishing a hobby is like calling brain surgery a job.

> —Paul Schullery, *Mountain Time* (1984)

I carry fewer flies each year, and less gear. Each year I watch a little more, fish a little less. My expertise with a fly rod, such as it is, fails to improve much.

> —Christopher Camuto, *A Fly Fisherman's Blue Ridge* (1990)

More than to Fish

In these sad and ominous days of mad fortune,
chasing every patriotic, thoughtful citizen, whether he
fishes or not, should lament that we have not among
our countrymen more fishermen.
    —President Grover Cleveland, *Fishing and Shooting
Sketches* (1906)

The pull of earthly passions and the compelling,
spiraling course of rivers is a balancing act. I want
to feel my body as a river, with its tributaries to the
spine and alluvial streams coursing outward; a witness
trying to find her bearings, bearing witness to the
waters that hold her in thrall.
    —Ailm Travers, "Run-Off," *A Different Angle: Fly
Fishing Stories by Women* (1995)

One light-filled afternoon, while pondering the difference between humans and lizards, I noticed a flash of silver in the water, which marked the beginning of my life as a fish watcher.

—Le Anne Schreiber, "The Long Light," *Uncommon Waters* (1991)

You're in the middle of a beautiful stream on a sunny afternoon, feeling a cool breeze on your skin, seeing the mountains around you, hearing the trickling of the water—all of that gives you hope and allows you to believe that life really does have more to offer.

—Sergeant Brian Mancini, Interview by Tom Dickson, "Fishing for Serenity," *Montana Outdoors* (May/June 2011)

To say that it was all just a matter of catching fish would be like saying that astronomy is nothing more than noticing the stars.

—Harry Middleton, *The Earth Is Enough: Growing Up in a World of Flyfishing, Trout & Old Men* (1989)

More than to Fish

There was a code, and though it was mostly unspoken, I absorbed it early on. You always put all the trout back in the water alive except for a few to eat. You didn't count your trout or call attention to their size or weight. You took time to watch and enjoy seeing your partners catch trout.

—Howard Frank Mosher

Good as the fishing was, the talk was better.
—Ferris Greenslet, *Under the Bridge* (1943) (of days with John Buchan)

The poetry of the sport hooked me long before I learned the prose.
—Judy Muller, "By George, She's Got It!" *Sports Illustrated* (October 5, 1987)

1,001 Pearls of Fishing Wisdom

Fishing seems awfully insignificant at times, but for those of us who love it, fishing provides opportunities—opportunities to learn, to laugh, and to live . . .

—Ted Baechtold, "Learning Through Fishing," *Casting Currents* (October 26, 2011)

If people concentrated on the really important things in life there'd be a shortage of fishing poles.

—Doug Larson

We also own a little boat and I'm like a kid with it. I take off early in the morning, fishing rod in tow, and just drift about the ocean all day.

—Perry Como

. . . it is discipline in the equality of men—for all men are equal before fish.

—President Herbert Hoover

More than to Fish

. . . there are two distinct kinds of visits to tackle-
shops, the visit to buy tackle and the visit which may
be described as Platonic when, being for some reason
unable to fish, we look for an excuse to go in, and
waste a tackle dealer's time.
>
> —Arthur Ransome, "On Tackle Shops,"
> *Rod and Line* (1929)

Respect your quarry.
>
> —Paul Guernsey, *Beyond Catch & Release* (2011)

There don't have to be a thousand fish in a river; let
me locate a good one and I'll get a thousand dreams
out of him before I catch him—and if I catch him, I'll
turn him loose.
>
> — Jim Deren, quoted in *Where the Pools Are Bright
> and Deep* by Dana Lamb (1973)

BIBLIOGRAPHY

ARTICLES

Alexson, Gustave. "Fresh Fish, Frozen Angler." *The New York Times*, March 11, 2010.

Apte, Stu. "World's Greatest Brown Trout Dry Fly Stream." *Field & Stream*, May 1972.

Babb, James R. "Around the Fire." *Gray's Sporting Journal*, February/March 2005.

———. "Home Away From Home." *Gray's Sporting Journal*, May/June 2005.

Baechtold, Ted. "Learning Through Fishing." *Casting Currents*, October 26, 2011.

Beckstorm, Kurt. "Fishing Resolutions for 2012." *North American Fisherman*, December 30, 2011.

Boyle, Robert H. "The Men Who Lived Two Lives in One." *Sports Illustrated*, April 29, 1968, 68–70.

Breining, Greg. "Wintertime, and Fishing is Easy." *The New York Times*, February 15, 2008. http://travel.nytimes.com/2008/02/15/travel/escapes/15icehouse.html?.

Brownlee, John. "Change of Pace." *Saltwater Sportsman*, February 9, 2012.

Bibliography

Bryson, Buzz. "Making the Speed Cast." *Fly Rod & Reel*, January 2007.

Cameron, Angus. "What Burns My Ass." *Outside Magazine*, July 1, 2000.

Cleveland, Stephen Grover. "Defense of Fishermen." *Saturday Evening Post*, October 19, 1901.

Davis, Julia. "Twenty Questions with Fishing Legends Ronald and Al Lindner." *Walleye Central*, 2011. http://www.walletecentral.com/articles/?a=2558.

Dickson, Tom. "Fishing for Serenity." *Montana Outdoors*, May–June 2011.

Duncan, David James. "A Manifesto for Ignorance." *Outside Magazine*, July 1, 2000.

Egan, D'Arcy. "A. K. Rates 'Best' in Fly Fishing World." *Cleveland.com*, January 10, 2008. http://blog.cleveland.com/sports/2008/01/ak_rates_best_in_fly_fishing_w.html.

Fanning, Dierdre. "Casting a Line, Catching Yourself." *The New York Times*, June 7, 2002. http://nytimes.com/2002/06/07/travel/journeys-casting-a-line-Catching-yourself.html.

Frazier, Ian. "Lighten Up." *Outside Magazine*, July 1, 2000.

Gibbs, Jerry. "Backup Plans Be Prepared to Catch Whatever Will Bite." *Outdoor Life*. http://www.outdoorlife.com/node/45583.

———. "Fishing's Top 40." *Outdoor Life*, September 2007. http://www.outdoorlife.com/node/45309.

Bibliography

Gorman, James. "A Rite That Bonds the Generations." *The New York Times*, June 22, 2001.http://www.nytimes.com/2001/06/22/arts/the-outsider-a-rite-that-bonds-the-generations.html.

Hemingway, Ernest. "Marlin off the Morro: A Cuban Letter." *Esquire*, Autumn 1933.

———. "On the Blue Water: A Gulf Stream Letter." *Esquire*, April 1936.

———. "Tuna Fishing in Spain." *Toronto Star Weekly*, February 18, 1922.

Hilton, Frank. "Shore Fishing Frustrations." *Free Bass Lures*, January 9, 2012. http://www.freebasslures.com/ShoreFishingFrustrations.htm.

Huff, Greg. "Huff's Post: Fish Don't Know Who's On the Other End of the Line." *North American Fishermen*, October 19, 2011.

Humphrey, William. "Tumult on a Wild Shore." *Sports Illustrated*, November 7, 1977, 42–4.

Johnson, W. H. "The Inveterate Angler." *Field & Stream*, May 1909, 177.

Jones, Allen. *Big Sky Journal*, vol. VIII, 74.

Kaminsky, Peter. "Trout Fresh from the Sea at the End of the Earth in Argentina." *The New York Times*, May 20, 2009. http://travel.nytimes.com/2009/05/24/travel/24explorer.html.

Kelly, Webb J. "Day Dreams." *The American Angler*, May 1921, 1–3.

Bibliography

Knight, Wendy. "A Tippy Test for Anglers: Landing Fish from a Kayak." *The New York Times*, September 9, 2005. http://travel.nytimes.com/2005/09/09/travel/escapes/09kayak.html.

Kreh, Lefty. Interview with Dave Jamieson. *Washington Post*, September 19, 2010.

Leeson, Ted. "The Best of Times, the Worst of Times." *Gray's Sporting Journal*, April 2008.

McLoughlin, W. Hardback. "Decisions." *Field & Stream*, August 1994, 28–9.

Mize, Jim. "Night-Fishing Tips." *Field & Stream*, February 1992, 24.

Muller, Judy. "By George, She's Got It!" *Sports Illustrated*, October 5, 1987, 86–8.

O'Neil, Paul. "Excalibur: The Steelhead." *Sports Illustrated*, March 11, 1957, 58.

O'Rourke, P. J. "A Fly Fishing Primer." *Sports Illustrated*, July 31, 1989.

Perry, Buck. "Fish Doctors: A Generation of Hard-to-Catch Bass." *Outdoor Life*, March 14, 2012.

Rauschenberger, Mark. "Humbling Reminder." *This Is Fly*, April/May 2012.

Robinson, Jerome B. "Jerry's Tips." *Field & Stream*, July 2005, 38.

Rupe, Old. "Prosit!" *Fly Anglers Online*. http://www.flyanglersonline.com/features/oldflies/part45.php.

Ryan, Will. "Rivers of Bronze." *Field & Stream*, July 2005, 68–9.

Bibliography

Scheck, Art. *Warmwater Fly Fishing Magazine*, 1998.

Schullery, Paul. "A Dreadful Scourge." *American Angler*, December 8, 2010.

Shacochis, Bob. "How to Eat a Fish." *Outside Magazine*, July 1, 2000.

Shaw, Hank. "Man, Nature, and Trout: Our Vanishing Traditions." *Atlantic*, April 12, 2011.

Sifton, Sam. "Silent Days on the Sea." *The New York Times*, March 28, 2010.

Simpson, Jeff. "One Recipe Worth Duplicating." *In-Fisherman*, December 7, 2011.

Skorupa, Joe. "Big Event, Small Fish." *Popular Mechanics*, December 1987.

Sternberg, Dick. "Fishing's Top 40."*Outdoor Life.* http://www.outdoor-life.com/node/45309.

"Stone. Water. Insect. Fish. Sunlight." *Los Angeles Times*, April 20, 2004. http://www.latimes.com/features/la-os-anthology20apr20,0,777477,full.story.

Stringfellow, Barry. "Strange Allure of Surf Fishing." *Yankee Magazine*, July/August 2007. http://www.yankeemagazine.com/issues/2007-07/interact/10things/surffishing/all.

Stuart, Walter. "Fishing Rules." *The New York Times*, January 29, 2012. www.nytimes.com/2012/01/30/nyregion/fishing-rules-a-different-sort-of-nun-and-other-nytimescom-reader-tales.html?_r=0.

Bibliography

Tapply, William. "Counting Coup." *American Angler*, December 8, 2010.

———. "Trout Fishing in the Battenkill River." *Yankee Magazine*,
September/October 2007. http://www.yankeemagazine.com/
issues/2007-09/interact/10things/battenkill.

Tomelleri, Joseph. "The Greatest Fish You've Never Seen." *Montana
Outdoors*, July/August 2002.

Trueblood, Ted. "Faith Hope and Success." *Field & Stream*, February
1961.

Ureneck, Lou. "Born the Fish: A South Jersey Boy's Life." *The New York
Times*, September 7, 2007.

Vincent, Dick. "Why Montana Went Wild." *Montana Outdoors*, May/
June 2004.

White, Ellington. "Striped Bass and Southern Solitude." *Sports
Illustrated*, October 10, 1966, 60–70.

BOOKS AND STORIES

Abott, Henry. *Fish Stories*. New York: 1919.

Abrames, Ken. *The Perfect Fish: Illusions in Fly Tying*. Portland, OR:
Frank Amato Publications, 1999.

Ackermann, Joan. "Ice Fishing." 1998.

Aelianus, Claudius. *On the Nature of Animals*. Rome, third century A.D.

Bibliography

Aksakov, Sergei. *Notes of Fishing* (1847), translated by Thomas P. Hodge. Evanston, IL: Northwestern University Press, 1997.

Allan, P. B. M. *Trout Heresy.* New York: Scribner, 1936.

Anderson, Sheridan. *The Curtis Creek Manifesto.* Portland, OR: Frank Amato Publications, 1978.

Atherton, John. *The Fly and the Fish.* New York: Macmillan, 1951.

Babcock, Havilah. "When a Lady Undresses." 1947

Babson, Stanley M. *Bonefishing.* New York: Harper & Row, 1965.

Bailey, John. *Reflections on the Water's Edge.* Ramsbury, UK: Crowood Press, 1987.

Baker, R. Palmer, Jr. *The Sweet of the Year.* New York: William Morrow, 1965.

Barich, Bill. *The Sporting Life: Horses, Boxers, Rivers, and a Russian Ballclub.* New York: Lyons Press, 1999.

Baron, Frank P. *What Fish Don't Want You to Know: An Insider's Guide to Freshwater Fishing.* New York: McGraw Hill, 2003.

Bates, H. E. *Gone Fishing: An Anthology of Fishing Stories.* London: Michael O'Mara Books, 1995.

Bean, Leon L. *Hunting, Fishing, and Camping.* Freeport, ME: Dingley Press, 1942.

Behnke, Robert. "Wild Trout and Native Trout—Is There a Difference?" *In Praise of Wild Trout.* Guilford, CT: Lyons Press, 1998.

Bibliography

Bergman, Ray. "Ray Bergman Says Goodbye." *Fishing with Ray Bergman.* New York: Alfred A. Knopf, 1970.

———. *Trout.* New York: Alfred A. Knopf, 1952.

Berners, Dame Juliana. *The Book of St. Albans.* St. Albans, UK: St. Albans Press, 1486.

———. *The Treatyse of Fishing with an Angle.* 1496.

Best, A. K. *Fly Fishing with A. K.* Mechanicsburg, PA: Stackpole Books, 2005.

Betts, John. Foreword to *The Fly Fisher's Craft: The Art and History* by Darrel Martin. Guilford, CT: Lyons Press, 2006.

Bialek, Janna. "Thoughts from a Fishing Past." *Uncommon Waters.* New York: Seal Press, 1991.

Black, George. *Casting a Spell: The Bamboo Fly Rod and the American Pursuit of Perfection.* New York: Random House, 2006.

Blackmore, R. D. "Crocker's Hole," *Slain by the Doones and Other Stories.* New York: Mead and Company, 1895.

Blaisdel, Harold F. *The Philosophical Fisherman.* Boston: Houghton Mifflin, 1969.

Blunt, Wilfred S. *A New Pilgrimage.* London: Kegan Paul, Trench & Co.,1889.

Bourne, Wade. *Basic Fishing: A Beginner's Guide.* New York: Skyhorse Publishing, 2011.

Bibliography

Boyle, Robert H. *Dapping: The Exciting Way of Fishing Flies that Fly, Quiver and Jump*. Mechanicburgs, PA: Stackpole Books, 2007.

———. *Fishing Giants and Other Men of Derring-Do*. Guilford, CT: Lyons Press, 2001.

Brautigan, Richard. *Trout Fishing in America*. San Francisco: Four Seasons Foundation, 1967.

Brooks, Joe. *Bass Bug Fishing*. New York: A. S. Barnes & Co., 1947.

Bunyan, John. *Pilgrim's Progress*. London: 1678.

Burroughs, John. *Locusts and Wild Honey*. London: Hamilton, Adams, & Co., 1879.

———. *Pepacton*. Cambridge: Riverside Press, 1881.

Burton, Mallory. *Uncommon Waters*. New York: Seal Press, 1991.

———. "Green River Virgins." *Green River Virgins: And Other Passionate Anglers*. Guilford, CT: Lyons Press, 2000.

Byron, Lord. *Don Juan*. 1818.

Camp, Raymond R. Introduction to *Art Flick's New Streamside Guide to Naturals and their Limitations*. Guilford, CT: Lyons Press, 2007.

Camp, Samuel G. *The Fine Art of Fishing*. New York: Outing Publishing Co., 1911.

Camuto, Christopher. "Caught by the Way." *In Praise of the Wild Trout*. New York: Lyons Press, 1998.

———. *A Fly Fisherman's Blue Ridge*. Athens: University of Georgia Press, 2001.

362

Bibliography

Carter, Jimmy. *An Outdoor Journal.* New York: Bantam Books, 1988.

Chalmers, Patrick R. *At the Tail of the Weir.* London: P. Allan, 1932.

———. "To An Old Friend." *Green Days and Blue Days.* Baltimore: The Norman, Remington Co., 1914.

Chatham, Russell. *Dark Waters.* New York: Clark City Press, 1988.

Chekhov, Anton. *The Seagull.* 1896.

Chesterton, Gilbert Keith. "A Fish Story." *The Collected Short Works of G. K. Chesterton.* San Francisco: Ignatius Press, 1986.

Clarke, Brian. *The Pursuit of the Stillwater Trout.* London: Adam & Charles Black, 1975.

Clarke, Brian & Goddard, John. *The Trout and the Fly.* New York: Doubleday, 1980.

Cleveland, Grover. *Fishing and Shooting Sketches.* New York: The Outing Publishing Co., 1906.

Cochrane, Alfred. "Fresh Run." *Collected Verses.* London: Longman, Greens, and Co., 1905.

Cole, John. *Fishing Came First.* New York: Lyons & Burford, 1989.

Coman, Dale Rex. *Pleasant River.* New York: W.W. Norton, 1966.

Connett, Eugene. *Any Luck?* New York: Windward House, 1933.

Cook, Beatrice. *Till Fish Do Us Part: The Confessions of a Fisherman's Wife.* New York: William Morrow, 1949.

Cotton, Charles. *The Compleat Angler* (Part 2). 1676.

Bibliography

Cunningham, Robert. *Chasing Records: An Angler's Quest.* New York: Skyhorse Publishing, 2012.

Dawson, George. "Fly Casting for Salmon." *Fishing with the fly: Sketches by lovers of the art* by Charles F. Orvis. Boston: Houghton, Mifflin, 1883.

Dennys, John. *The Secrets of Angling.* London, 1613.

Deren, Jim. Quoted in The Fish's Eye by Ian Frazier. New York: Farrar Straus Giroux, 2002.

———. Quoted in *Where the Pools Are Bright and Deep* by Dana Lamb. New York: Winchester Press, 1973.

DiBenedetto, David. *On the Run: An Angler's Journey Down the Striper Coast.* New York: William Morrow, 2005.

Dugger, Albia. "The Search for the Sword." *Uncommon Waters.* New York: Seal Press, 1991.

Dunne, J. W. *Sunshine and the Dry Fly.* London: Adam & Charles Black, 1924.

Edye, Huish. *The Angler and the Trout.* London: Adam & Charlies Black, 1945.

Eliot, George. *Middlemarch.* Edinburgh and London: William Black Wood & Sons, 1874.

———. *The Mill on the Floss.* Edinburgh and London: William Black Wood & Sons, 1860.

Bibliography

Ellis, Colin. "The Devout Angler." Quoted in *The Trout Fisherman's Bedside Book* by Arthur R. Macdougall, Jr. New York: Simon & Schuster, 1963.

Engle, Ed. *Fly Fishing the Tailwaters.* Harrisburg: Stackpole Books, 1991.

Engles, John. "Bullhead." *Big Water.* New York: Lyons & Burford, 1995.

Evanoff, Vlad. *2002 Fishing Tips and Tricks.* New York: Galahad Books, 1999.

Farson, Negley. *Going Fishing.* New York: Harcourt, Brace and Company, 1943.

Fedden, Romilly. *Golden Days.* London: Adam & Charles Black, 1919.

Fitch, Fitz James. "Sea Trout." *Fishing with the fly: by lovers of the art* by Charles F. Orvis. Troy, NY: H. B. Nims, 1883.

Fitzgerald, Mike, Jr. Foreword to *Fifty Places to Fish Before You Die* by Chris Santella. New York: Stewart, Tabori & Chang, 2004.

Flick, Art. *Art Flick's Streamside Guide to Naturals and Their Limitations.* New York: G. P. Putnam's Sons, 1947.

———. *Art Flick's New Streamside Guide to Naturals and Their Limitations.* Guilford, CT: Lyons Press, 2007.

Foote, John Taintor. *Change of Idols.* New York: Appleton-Century, 1935.

Ford, Corey & MacBain, Alastair. Introduction to *Trout Fishing* by Dan Holland. New York: T. Y. Crowell Co., 1949.

Bibliography

Fox, William Sherwood. *Silken Lines and Silver Hooks.* Toronto: Copp Clark, 1954.

Frazier, Ian. *The Fish's Eye: Essays about Angling and the Outdoors.* New York: Picador, 2002.

Garner, Lewis-Ann. "One for the Glass Case." *Uncommon Waters.* New York: Seal Press, 1991.

Gibbs, Jerry. *Bass Myths Exploded: Newest Ways to Catch Largemouths.* Philadelphia: McKay, 1978.

Gierach, John. *Another Lousy Day in Paradise.* New York: Simon & Schuster, 1996.

———. *Dances with Trout.* New York: Simon & Schuster, 1994.

———. *Fly Fishing in the High Country.* Mechanicsburg, PA: Stackpole Books, 2004.

———. *Trout Bum.* Boulder, CO: Pruett Publishing Company, 1986.

———. *The View from Rat Lake.* Boulder, CO: Pruett Publishing Company, 1988.

Gingrich, Arnold. *The Fishing in Print: A Guided Tour through Five Centuries of Angling Literature.* New York: Winchester Press, 1974.

———. *The Joys of Trout.* New York: Crown Publishers, 1973.

———. *The Well-Tempered Angler.* New York: Alfred A. Knopf, 1965.

Goddard, John. *John Goddard's Trout Fishing Techniques: Practical Fly Fishing Solutions.* New York: Lyons & Burford, 1996.

366

Bibliography

Gordon, Sid W. *How to Fish from Top to Bottom*. Mechanicsburg, PA: Stackpole Books, 1955.

Graves, John. *Goodbye to a River*. New York: Alfred A. Knopf, 1960.

Greenslet, Ferris. *Under the Bridge*. Boston: Houghton Mifflin, 1946.

Grey, Lord Edward, of Fallondon, *Fly-Fishing*. London: J. M. Dent & Co., 1899.

Guernsey, Paul. *Beyond Catch & Release*. New York: Skyhorse Publishing, 2011.

Guest, Edgar A. "A Boy and His Dad." *When Day is Done*. Chicago: Reilley & Lee Co., 1921.

———. "The Fishing Outfit." *Just Folks*. Chicago: Reilley & Lee, 1917.

———. "Out Fishin'." *The Path to Home*. Chicago: Reilley & Lee Co., 1919.

Hackle, Sparse Grey. "Murder." *Fishless Days, Angling Nights*. New York: Crown Publishing, 1971.

———. *Great Fishing Tackle Catalogs of the Golden Age*. Guilford, CT: Lyons Press, 1999.

———. "Night Fishing." *Fishless Days, Angling Nights*. New York: Crown Publishing, 1971.

———. "The Perfect Angler." *Fishless Days, Angling Nights*. New York: Crown Publishing, 1971.

Haig-Brown, Roderick L. *Gamest Fish of All*. 1956.

Bibliography

——. *A River Never Sleeps*. Machynlleth: Coch Y Bonddu Books, 1946.

Hall, John Inglis. *Fishing a Highland Stream*. New York: Viking, 1987.

Hamilton, Edward. *Recollections of fly fishing for salmon, trout, and grayling*. London: S. Marston, 1891.

Harrison, Jim. "Older Fishing." *Astream: American Writers on Fly Fishing*. New York: Skyhorse Publishing, 2012.

Harrop, Rene. "Encounter on the Flat." *Into the Backing: Incredible True Stories About the Big Ones that Got Away* by Lamar Underwood. Guilford, CT: Lyons Press, 2001.

——. *Trout Hunter: The Way of an Angler*. Boulder, CO: Pruett Publishing, 2003.

Hawker, Peter. *Instructions to Young Sportsmen*. 1814.

Hemingway, Ernest. "Big Two-Hearted River." *In Our Time*. New York: Boni & Liveright, 1925.

——. Santiago in *The Old Man and the Sea*. New York: Charles Scribner's Sons, 1952.

Hemingway, Jack. *A Life Worth Living: The Adventures of a Passionate Sportsman*. Guilford, CT: Lyons Press, 2002.

Hemingway, Lorian. "Walk on Water for Me." *A Different Angle: Fly Fishing Stories by Women*. New York: Seal Press, 1995.

——. "The Young Woman and the Sea." *Uncommon Waters*. New York: Seal Press, 1991.

Bibliography

Henshall, Dr. James A. *Book of the Black Bass*. Cincinnati: Robert Clark & Co., 1881.

Herbert, George. *Jacula Prudentum*. Edited by Barnabas Oley, 1651.

Herbert, W. H. (Frank Forester), *Fishes and Fishing*. 1850.

Hersey, John. *Blues*. New York: Alfred A. Knopf, 1987.

Hewitt, Edward R. *A Trout and Salmon Fisherman for Seventy-Five Years*. New York: Charles Scribner's Sons, 1948.

Hills, John Waller. *River Keeper: The Life of William James Lunn*. London: G. Bles, 1934.

———. *A Summer on the Test*. London: P. Allan, 1930.

Holmes, Oliver Wendell, Sr. "The Banker's Secret." *The Poetical Works of Oliver Wendell Holmes*. Boston: Houghton, Mifflin, 1850.

Holt, John. "Death on the Musselshell." *On Killing: Meditations on the Chase* by Robert F. Jones. Guilford, CT: Lyons Press, 2001.

Hoover, Herbert. *Fishing for Fun—And to Wash Your Soul*. New York: Random House, 1963.

Hordern, Michael. *Gone Fishing: An Anthology of Fishing Stories*. London: Michael O'Mara Books, 1995.

Houston, Pam. "The Company of Men." *A Different Angle: Fly Fishing Stories by Women*. New York: Seal Press, 1995.

Howitt, William. *The Rural Life in England*. London: Longman, Orme, Brown, Green, & Longmans, 1838.

Bibliography

Hughes, Dave. *Reading the Water: A Fly Fisher's Handbook for Finding Trout in All Types of Water*. Mechanicsburg, PA: Stackpole Books, 1988.

Humphrey, William. *My Moby Dick*. New York: Doubleday, 1978.

Humphreys, Joe. *Joe Humphreys's Trout Tactics*. Mechanicsburg, PA: Stackpole Books, 1981.

———. *On the Trout Stream with Joe Humphreys*. Mechanicsburg, PA: Stackpole Books, 1989.

Irving, Washington. *The Angler*. 1820.

Jardine, Charles. Foreword to *Dynamic Nymphing: Tactics, Techniques, and Flies from Around the World* by George Daniel. Mechanicsburg, PA: Stackpole Books, 2011.

Jeffries, Norman. "Ketchin' Pick'rel." *Fisherman's Verse*. New York: Duffield & Company, 1919.

Jennings, Luke. *Blood Knots*. London: Atlantic Books, 2011.

Jensen, Albert C. *The Cod*. New York: Crowell, 1972.

Jordan, David Starr. *Fish Stories, Alleged and Experienced*. New York: H. Holt & Company, 1909.

Juracek, John & Mathews, Craig. *Fishing Yellowstone Hatches*. Guilford, CT: Lyons Press, 1992.

Kaminsky, Peter. *The Fly Fisherman's Guide to the Meaning of Life*. New York: Skyhorse Publishing, 2008.

Keene, J. H. *The Practical Fisherman*. London: The Bazaar Office, 1881.

Bibliography

Kelson, George M. *The Salmon Fly*. London: Wyman & Sons, 1895.

Kipling, Rudyard. "Kipling to James M. Conland, 8 august 1899," in *The Letters of Rudyard Kipling*, edited by Thomas Pinney. Iowa City: University of Iowa Press, 1990.

Kite, Oliver. *Nymph Fishing in Practice*. London: Jenkins, 1963.

Knight, John Alden. *Black Bass*. New York: G. P. Putnam's Sons, 1949.

———. *Field Book of Fresh-Water Angling*. New York: G. P. Putnam's Sons, 1944.

Kreh, Lefty. *Lefty Kreh's Presenting the Fly: A Practical Guide to the Most Important Element of Fly Fishing*. Guilford, CT: Lyons Press, 1999.

———. *Lefty Kreh's Ultimate Guide to Fly Fishing: Everything Anglers Need to Know*. Guilford, CT: Lyons Press, 2003.

Kuss, Mary S. "Jesus, Pete, It's a Woman Fly Fishing." *Uncommon Waters*. New York: Seal Press, 1991.

La Branche, George M. L. *The Dry Fly and Fast Water*. New York: Charles Scribner's Sons, 1914.

LaFontaine, Gary. Foreword to *Trout Bum* by John Gierach. New York: Simon & Schuster, 1986.

Lampman, Ben Hur. *A Leaf from French Eddy*. New York: Harper & Row, 1965.

Lang, Andrew. Introduction to Walton's *The Compleat Angler*. London: J. M. Dent & Co., 1906.

Lapsley, Peter. *River Trout Flyfishing*. London: Unwin Hyman, 1988.

Bibliography

Lawrie, W. H. *A Reference Book of English Trout Flies*. London: Pelham, 1967.

Leeson, Ted. Foreword to *The Fly Fisher's Craft: The Art and History* by Darrel Martin. Guilford, CT: Lyons Press, 2006.

———. Introduction to *The Fly Fisher's Craft: The Art and History* by Darrel Martin. Guilford, CT: Lyons Press, 2006.

———. *The Habit of Rivers*. Guilford, CT: Lyons Press, 1994.

———. *Inventing Montana: Dispatches from the Madison Valley*. New York: Skyhorse Publishing, 2009.

———. *Jerusalem Creek*. Guilford, CT: Lyons Press, 2002.

Legler, Gretchen. "Fishergirl." *A Different Angle: Fly Fishing Stories by Women*. New York: Seal Press, 1995.

Livermore, Jesse. Quoted in *Come Into My Trading Room* by Alexander Elder. New York: John Wiley & Sons, 2002.

Livingston, A. D. *Fishing for Bass*. Philadelphia: Lippincott, 1974.

Lord, Nancy. "Magadan Luck." *Uncommon Waters*. New York: Seal Press, 1991.

Lowell, Amy. "The Trout." *A Dome of Many-Coloured Glass*. Boston: Houghton Mifflin, 1912.

Lyly, John. *Euphues*. London: 1578.

Macdougall, Arthur R, Jr. *The Trout Fisherman's Bedside Book*. New York: Simon & Schuster, 1963.

Bibliography

Maclean, Norman. *A River Runs Through It*. Chicago: University of Chicago Press, 1976.

Marinaro, Vincent C. *In the Ring of the Rise*. New York: Crown Publishing, 1976.

Marshall, Howard. *Reflections on a River*. London: H. F. & G. Witherby, 1967.

Martin, Darrel. *The Fly Fisher's Craft: The Art and History*. Guilford, CT: Lyons Press, 2006.

Mather, Fred. "Big-Mouth Black Bass." *Songs for Fishermen*. Cincinnati: Stewart Kidd Company, 1922.

———. *My Angling Friends*. New York: Forest and Stream Publishing Company, 1901.

Mathews, Craig. *Western Fly-Fishing Strategies*. Guilford, CT: Lyons Press, 1998.

Maxwell, Jessica. "Twelve Flew into the Cuckoo's Nest." *A Different Angle: Fly Fishing Stories by Women*. New York: Seal Press, 1995.

McClane, A. J. *The Compleat McClane*, edited by John Merwin. New York: E. P. Dutton, 1988.

McClane, A. J. "Song of the Angler." *Field & Stream*, 1967.

McDonald, John. Introduction to *The Complete Fly Fisherman*. New York: Charles Scribner's Sons, 1947.

McGuane, Thomas. *The Longest Silence*. New York: Alfred A. Knopf, 1999.

Bibliography

———. *An Outside Chance*. Bath, UK: Chivers Press, 1990.

———. In *Silent Seasons*, edited by Russell Chatham. New York: E. P. Dutton, 1978.

———. Foreword to *Spring Creeks* by Mike Lawson. Mechanicsburg, PA: Stackpole Books, 2003.

McNally, Tom. *The Complete Book of Fly Fishing*. Camden, ME: Ragged Mountain Press, 1993.

Mengel, Robert M. *Fly Fisherman's Odyssey*. New York: Lyons & Burford, 1993.

Meyers, Steven J. *San Juan River Chronicle*. Guilford, CT: Lyons Press, 1994.

Middleton, Harry. *The Earth is Enough: Growing Up in a World of Flyfishing, Trout & Old Men*. Boulder, CO: Pruett Publishing, 1989.

———. *Rivers of Memory*. Boulder, CO: Pruett Publishing, 1993.

Milton, Leroy. "Getting out the Fly Books." *Angling*. New York: Charles Scribner's Sons, 1897.

Moir, Allison. "Love the Man, Love the Fly Rod." *A Different Angle: Fly Fishing Stories by Women*. New York: Seal Press, 1995.

Morris, Holly, Ed. *A Different Angle: Fly Fishing Stories by Women*. New York: Seal Press, 1995.

Morris, Joseph. "Fish Stories." *Songs for Fishermen*. Cincinnati: Stewart Kidd Company, 1922.

Bibliography

Muller, Judy. "Only One Fly." *A Different Angle: Fly Fishing Stories by Women*. New York: Seal Press, 1995.

Nelson, Kevin. *The Angler's Book of Daily Inspiration*. New York: McGraw-Hill, 1997.

Norris, Thaddeus. *The American Angler's Book*. Philadelphia: E. H. Butler, 1864.

Ohman, Jack. *Fear of Fly Fishing*. New York: Simon & Schuster, 1988.

Ovid, *Ars Amatoria*. 2 A.D.

Owell, George. *Coming Up for Air*. London: Secker and Warburg, 1939.

Page, Margot. *Little Rivers*. Guilford, CT: Lyons Press, 1995.

———. "The Island." *The Gigantic Book of Fishing Stories*. New York: Skyhorse Publishing, 2007.

Palmer, Tom. "Trout Habitat in the Blackfoot Country." *In Praise of Wild Trout*. Guilford, CT: Lyons Press, 1988.

Patterson, Neil. *Chalkstream Chronicle*. New York: Lyons & Burford, 1995.

Penn, Richard. *The Angler's Weekend Book*. 1833.

———. *Maxims and Hints for an Angler and Miseries of Fishing*. London: J. Murray, 1833.

Perry, Bliss. *Fishing with a Worm*. Boston: Houghton, Mifflin, 1904.

Pertwee, Roland. "The River God." *The Saturday Evening Post*, July 7, 1928.

Bibliography

Philpott, Lindsey. *The Complete Book of Fishing Knots, Leaders, and Lines*. New York: Skyhorse Publishing, 2008.

Pickney, Frank S. "Winter Angling." *Fishing with the fly, Sketches by lovers of the art* by Charles F. Orvis. Boston: Houghton, Mifflin, 1883.

Platts, William Carter. *Angling Done Here!* London: Jarrold, 1897.

Plunket-Green, Harry. *Where the Bright Waters Meet*. New York: Allan, 1936.

Prime, W. C. *I Go A-Fishing*. New York: Harper & Brothers, 1873.

Proulx, Annie. *The Shipping News*. New York: Simon & Schuster, 1993.

Raines, Howell. *Fly Fishing Through the Midlife Crisis*. New York: HarperCollins, 1993.

Randolph, John. Foreword to *Trout Hunter: The Way of an Angler* by Rene Harrop. Boulder, CO: Pruett Publishing, 2003.

Ransom, Elmer. *Fishing's Just Luck*. New York: Howell, Soskin, 1945.

Ransome, Arthur. *Rod and Line*. London: Jonathan Cape, 1929.

Raymond, Steve. *The Year of the Angler*. New York: Winchester Press, 1973.

———. *The Year of the Trout*. Seattle: Sasquatch Books, 1995.

Ristori, Al. *The Complete Book of Surf Fishing*. New York: Skyhorse Publishing, 2008.

Ritz, Charles. *A Fly Fisher's Life*. New York: Holt, 1959.

Robb, James. *Notable Angling Literature*. London: H. Jenkins, 1946.

Bibliography

Rosenbauer, Tom. *The Orvis Guide to Beginning Fly Fishing*. New York: Skyhorse Publishing, 2009.

Ruark, Robert. *The Old Man and the Boy*. Boston: G. K. Hall, 1957.

Rubin, Louis D., Jr. *The Even-Tempered Angler*. Piscataway, NJ: Winchester Press, 1983.

Salmon, M. H. "Dutch." *The Catfish as Metaphor*. Silver City, NM: High-Lonesome Books, 1997.

Sawyer, Frank. *Keeper of the Stream*. London: Adam & Charles Black, 1952.

Scheck, Art. *A Fishing Life is Hard Work*. Mechanicsburg, PA: Stackpole Books, 2003.

Schreiber, Le Anne. "The Long Light." *Uncommon Waters*. New York: Seal Press, 1991.

———. *Midstream*. New York: Lyons & Burford, 1990.

———. "Predilections." *On Killing: Meditations on the Chase* by Robert F. Jones. Guilford, CT: Lyons Press, 2001.

Schullery, Paul. *Mountain Time*. New York: Schocken Books, 1984.

Schwiebert, Ernest G., Jr. "Memories of Michigan."

———. *Trout*. New York: E. P. Dutton, 1978.

———. "Twelve Lessons for a Trout-Fishing Friend." 1971.

Shakespeare, William. *Twelfth Night* (c. 1601)

Shepherd, Jean. "Hairy Gertz and the Forty-Seven Crappies." *In God We Trust, All Others Pay Cash*. New York: Doubleday, 1966.

Bibliography

Shepherd, Odell. *Thy Rod and Thy Creel*. Hartford, CT: E. V. Mitchell, 1930.

Sheringham, H. T. *Coarse Fishing*. London: Adam & Charles Black, 1912.

———. *Fishing: Its Cause, Treatment, and Cure* (c. 1912)

Skues, G. E. M. *Itchen Memories*. London: H. Jenkins, 1951.

———. *Minor Tactics of the Chalk Stream*. London: Adam & Charles Black, 1910.

———. "Mr. Theodore Castwell." *Sidelines, Sidelights, and Reflections*. 1947.

———. *The Way of a Trout with a Fly*. London: Adam & Charles, 1921.

Smith, Jennifer. "Cheeseballs and Emergers." *A Different Angle: Fly Fishing Stories by Women*. New York: Seal Press, 1995.

———. "Paul Bunyan: My Wooly Bugger Chucking Machine." *Uncommon Waters*. New York: Seal Press, 1991.

Smith, Pat. "Old Iron Jaw." *Lamar Underwood's Bass Almanac*. New York: Doubleday, 1979.

Sojourner, Sabrina. "Currents." *Uncommon Waters*. New York: Seal Press, 1991.

Stanton, Frank L. "A Fisherman in Town." *Songs for Fishermen*. London: Stewart Kidd Company, 1922.

Steinbeck, John. *America and Americans*. New York: Viking Press, 1966.

Bibliography

Sutcliffe, Tom. *Reflections on Flyfishing*. South Africa: Mark & Ronald Basel, 1990.

Sutton, Keith. *The Crappie Fishing Handbook*. New York: Skyhorse Publishing, 2012.

Swegman, Ron P. "The Old Line" (short story). 2010.

Tabory, Lou. *Inshore Fly Fishing*. Guilford, CT: Lyons Press, 1992.

Tapply, H. G. *The Sportsman's Notebook*. New York: Holt, Rinehart and Winston, 1964.

Tapply, William. *A Fly-Fishing Life*. Guilford, CT: Lyons Press, 1997.

Taverner, Eric. *Trout Fishing from All Angles*. London: Seeley, Service and Company, 1929.

Taverner, Eric & Moore, John. "Thoughts." *The Angler's Weekend Book*. London: Seeley, Service and Company, 1949.

Tennyson, Alfred. "The Brook." *Enoch Arden and Other Poems*. Boston: J.E. Tilton, 1862.

Thompson, Leslie P. *Fishing in New England*. New York: Van Nostrand, 1955.

Thoreau, Henry David. "Ktaadn." *The Maine Woods*. Boston: Ticknor and Fields, 1864.

———. *Walden*. Boston: Ticknor and Fields, 1854.

Tolstoy, Leo. *Anna Karenina*. Moscow: Russian Messenger, 1877.

Traver, Robert. *Anatomy of a Fisherman*. Santa Barbara: Peregrine Smith, 1978.

Bibliography

————. *Trout Madness*. New York: St. Martin's Press, 1960.

Travler, Ailm. "Fly Fishing Folly." *Uncommon Waters*. New York: Seal Press, 1991.

————. "Run-Off." *A Different Angle: Fly Fishing Stories by Women*. New York: Seal Press, 1995.

Twain, Mark. *Roughing It*. Hartford, CT: American Publishing Company, 1872.

Van de Water, F. F. *In Defense of Worms*. New York: Duell, Sloan and Pearce, 1949.

Van Dyke, Henry. "The Angler's Reveille." *The Poems of Henry Van Dyke*. New York: Charles Scribner's Sons, 1911.

————. "An Angler's Wish in Town" (poem). 1894.

Voss Bark, Conrad. *A Fly on the Water*. London: Allen & Unwin, 1986.

Walden Howard T, II. *Upstream and Down*. New York: Macmillan & Co., 1938.

Walton, Izaak. *The Compleat Angler*. London: Ward, Lock & Co., 1653.

Weber, Katharine. "Without a Backward Cast." *Uncommon Waters*. New York: Seal Press, 1991.

Weeks, Edward. *Fresh Waters*. Boston: Little, Brown, 1968.

Wetherell, W. D. *This American River: Five Centuries of Writing About the Connecticut River*. Lebanon, NH: The University Press of New England, 2002.

————. *Vermont River*. Piscataway, NJ: Winchester Press, 1984.

Bibliography

Wheatly, Hewitt. *The Rod and Line*. London: Longman, Brown, Green & Longmans, 1849.

Wilson, Dermot. *Fishing the Dry Fly*. London: Adam & Charles Black, 1970.

Wright, Leonard M., Jr. *Fishing the Dry Fly as a Living Insect*. New York: Dutton, 1972.

———. *Fly Fishing Heresies*. New York: Winchester Press, 1975.

———. *The Ways of Trout*. New York: Winchester Press, 1985.

Wulff, Joan. *Joan Wulff's Fly-Fishing: Expert Advice from a Woman's Perspective*. Mechanicsburg, PA: Stackpole Books, 1991.

Wulff, Lee. *Fishing with Lee Wulff*, edited by Edward C. Janes. New York: Alfred A. Knopf, 1972.

———. Foreword to *The Atlantic Salmon*. New York: Lyons & Burford, 1983.

———. *Lee Wulff's Handbook of Freshwater Fishing*. New York: Frederick A. Stokes Co., 1939.

Younger, John. *River Angling for Salmon and Trout*. Edinburgh: William Blackwood & Sons, 1840.

Zern, Ed. *Are Fishermen People?* New York: Harper & Bros., 1951.

———. "The Ethics, Perhaps, of Fly Fishing." *Fifty Years of Ed Zern*. Guilford, CT: Lyons Press, 2003.

Bibliography

———. *How to Tell Fish from Fishermen*. New York: Daniel Appleton-Century Co., 1947.

———. *To Hell with Fishing*. New York: Daniel Appleton-Century Co., 1945.

WEB

Baughman, Dan. "Fishing, Spirituality and Us." *Bow Narrows* (blog), February 16, 2012. http://bownarrows.blogspot.com/2012/02/fishing-spirituality-and-us.html.

Bush, George H. W. "Message on the Observance of National Fishing Week, June 5–11, 1989." *The American Presidency Project*, June 7, 1989. http://www.presidency.ucsb.edu/ws/?pid=17123.

Daughton, Tim. "Layering for Warmth and Comfort." *Orvis News* (blog), December 20, 2011. http://www.orvisnews.com/FlyFishing/Repost-Layering-for-Warmth-and-Comfort.aspx.

Eisenkramer, Rabbi Eric. "Fly Fishing and Frustration." *The Fly Fishing Rabbi* (blog), January 17, 2011. http://theflyfishingrabbi.blogsport.com/2007/06/fly-fishing-frustration-fly-fishing-is.html.

———. "Fly Fishing in Argentina." *The Fly Fishing Rabbi* (blog), January 5, 2008. http://theflyfishingrabbi.blogsport.com/2008/01/fly-fishing-in-argentina-in-december-my.html.

Bibliography

Eldridge, Bryan. "6 Things Guides Do That You Shouldn't." *Orvis News* (blog), November 11, 2011. http://www.orvisnews.com/FlyFishing/ What-guides-do-that-you-shouldnt.aspx.

McPherson, Austin. "The Gorge." *Fly Rod & Reel Online* (blog), October 29, 2008. http://www.flyrodreel.com/blogs/austinmcpherson/2008/ october/the-gorge.

Monohan, Phil. "5 Keys to Stealth." *Orvis News* (blog), April 4, 2012. http://www.orvisnews.com/FlyFishing/Repose-5-Keys-to-Sealth. aspx.

———. "The Agony and the Ecstasy." *Orvis News* (blog), April 2, 2012. http://www.orvisnews.com/FlyFishg/The-Agony-and-the-Ectasy. aspx.

Those Quoted

Those Quoted

Those Quoted

Those Quoted

387

Those Quoted

Those Quoted

389

Those Quoted